Marketing for Non-Marketing Managers

■

BEEVERS CONSULTING LTD.
180 HORNINGLOW STREET
BURTON ON TRENT
DE14 1NG
TEL: 0283 515551
FAX: 0283 515556

Marketing for Non-Marketing Managers

PATRICK FORSYTH

the Institute
of Management

PITMAN PUBLISHING

Pitman Publishing
128 Long Acre, London WC2E 9AN

A Division of Longman Group UK Limited

First published in 1993

© Longman Group UK Limited 1993

A CIP catalogue record for this book can be obtained
from the British Library

ISBN 0 273 60141 5

Photoset in Linotron Century Schoolbook by
Northern Phototypesetting Co., Ltd., Bolton
Printed and bound by Bell and Bain Ltd., Glasgow

For my Father
(the ultimate non-marketing person)

'They say if you build a better mousetrap than your neighbour, people are going to come running. They are like hell! It's marketing that makes the difference.'

ED JOHNSON

Contents

■

Foreword

■

If marketing is so important,
how is it so few people understand it?

There are two main reasons for writing this book. The first is that, during some 20 years of working in marketing, I have been regularly surprised by how many people misunderstand what it is all about. On numerous occasions if asked what I do, a reply that I am in marketing has led initially to confusion. Other people do not have this problem. If a dentist, say, is asked what he does, people understand; they may not like the thought of it, but they understand. In a company too the function of many is clear to all; the production manager keeps the production line moving; a secretary types the letters and sends out the invoices (yes, and much, much more); and the accountant keeps the score.

In addition, mention marketing and it conjures up all the wrong images. It is, well, sort of . . . advertising; or selling. The sort of selling which forces unsuitable goods on reluctant customers. Market traders, 'Brand X', supermarkets and too much 'junk mail' are all examples of the kind of things that seem to come to mind. Why is this? Marketing people believe marketing is important; if it is, then other people should know about it. Manifestly marketing people are not always too good at explaining away the confusion. Indeed in some companies their image does not help. Marketing people are sometimes seen as spending too much money, and too long at lunch; salesmen are seen as gadding about in company cars to no good purpose and advertising people are seen as creative deviants who earn too much money by far.

Does all this matter? Yes, I believe it does, because so many people in any company are, in fact, actually involved in marketing in some way, whether they see it or not. This is true from the top to the bottom of the organisation. Marketing may be a top management responsibility, yet it involves many throughout the operation, in every department and at every level. There are many who should have a clear view of what marketing is and how the marketing process works, not only because it is at the heart of how any commercial organisation works and they may well find it interesting, but also because it impinges on their job and *vice versa*.

So, contributing to the reduction of this confusion and being able to play a part in demonstrating the importance and relevance of marketing to a range of people around the company was attractive. More so because, as the rest of this text aims to demonstrate, a better understanding can, I believe, contribute in a practical way to a company's success.

You may recall that this section began with reference to two main reasons for writing this book, and wonder what the other one is. Although primarily a consultant and trainer, writing is part of the portfolio of services from which I make my living – so my writing this book, about marketing, is itself a result of my own marketing activity and, in turn, your reading it is a result of the publisher's marketing activity. So it is definitely an important process.

Preface

∎

Whatever job you do within the organisation for which you work, it could be it is even more important than you think. Why? Because any commercial organisation only succeeds if it can be not just financially viable, but profitable. And profits come from the market; from customers. The process known as marketing, which this book reviews, is, at its simplest, the process of ensuring that sufficient customers do business with an organisation and come back for more, to ensure its profitability. If your job assists, even obliquely, with this process, it is vital. Everything that is part of marketing or links to it contributes in some way to company success.

By way of example, consider the following situation which I came across in a company selling office stationery products. The Administration Manager, concerned to speed up the way in which incoming calls were dealt with at the switchboard, had instructed the operator to respond to a variety of customer enquiries and queries by asking 'Are you placing an order, or chasing an order?' (the two being dealt with by different departments). Well intentioned no doubt, but the net result was that it was suggested to every caller that orders *needed* to be chased. A small point perhaps, but one where two people at different levels act without due regard to the customer and the impression they will have of the organisation. And customer service is inseparable from marketing.

So, whatever your role, this book aims to provide important information. You may be new to the commercial role; you may be well experienced but in only one particular aspect of the business, in production, finance, or computer services say; you may be in the early stages of a marketing career, or working in one particular aspect of the activity, perhaps sales, customer service, research, or account management – or both. Whatever your role you need to know about marketing.

This book will help demystify marketing (it is much misunderstood, and is not, as is sometimes assumed, a euphemism for advertising or selling – though these are both important and thus produce the longest chapters); it explains marketing and, more important, it shows how the disparate techniques of marketing work together and act to produce the commercial success the enterprise seeks. It also indicates how its task affects, and is affected by, other functions and departments (the *boxed* examples make this point progressively throughout the text). Thus the emphasis is on those aspects which are either most visible or most likely to overlap with other areas, rather than on those areas necessarily coped with by marketing people alone.

An understanding of, and respect for, marketing amongst those throughout any organisation is not simply a 'good thing'; it is practically useful and important. The most important people in any business are its customers. Satisfying them is paramount, their degree of satisfaction will be reflected in the degree to which a company prospers. An organisation where *everyone* in any way concerned, through their work and activities, with the customer – however seemingly indirectly – has a real understanding of the importance of marketing will do better than its competitors who operate on a more introspective basis.

Marketing links the organisation with the outside world and, as we shall see, there is more to this than perhaps first meets the eye.

Patrick Forsyth   Spring 1993
Touchstone Training and Consultancy
17 Clocktower Mews
Arlington Avenue
London N1 7BB

Acknowledgements

■

Anyone who writes on business matters, particularly someone who works as a consultant and trainer as I do, may perhaps be forgiven for finding it difficult to acknowledge specific sources. Any ability I have to set out explanations such as those attempted in this book, comes from a plethora of past experiences; particularly from the involvements I have had over the years with many different clients and the delegates from whom I have learned so much on courses too numerous to mention.

Having written other books on sales and marketing topics I have drawn just a little on material appearing in some of them, and rather than acknowledging individual paragraphs or figures I would simply mention here that sources include:

Marketing Professional Services (also published by Pitman)
Running an Effective Sales Office (Gower Publishing)
Making Marketing Work (co-authored by Gerard Earls and published by Kogan Page)

All of these have rather different objectives to the present volume, but overlap in some way with the topic it presents.

Otherwise, I would offer a general thank you to all those who have played a part in getting me involved in the business of marketing in the first place, and helped develop the fascination and enthusiasm I have had for it ever since. If a little of this is passed on through this book to others perhaps less involved in marketing then it will have achieved something worthwhile.

P.F.

NOTE
Action and implementation

■

This is not intended to be an academic book. Its main aim is to demystify marketing and the marketing process and show what contribution it makes to the success and profitability of the organisation. In addition, it sets out to show how marketing interfaces with other departments and functions around the firm. At the end of the day this affects people; take the people away from any business and there is little meaningful left. For the reader that is you, your colleagues and those above and below you around the whole business.

A theme of the following pages is communication around the organisation as well as with the outside world; with the market. Without a doubt communication is going to be better, and more achieved as a result, if the parties communicating understand each other. As you read on you may well be prompted to think of certain overlaps between your role and that of your colleagues, indeed I hope this is the case. If so it may well be worth making a note of any action, discussion or review that you feel may help make either your job or that of a colleague proceed more effectively. After all friction is always potentially present when people work together in groups, and inevitably causes more heat than anything constructive.

To facilitate constructive thinking of this sort each chapter ends with a page designed to take notes (if you do not wish to mark the book you can devise something similar and separate). You may find it useful to note things as you read or review how marketing influences you at the end; the appendix is a further prompt to such a process.

1

Marketing in context
Introduction and definitions

Not only is marketing an area in which there is considerable jargon, it is itself a word which confuses because there is not one straightforward definition at all; the word is used in several different ways. All are broader in scope and complexity than the feeling amongst many that marketing is simply a grand word for advertising, or selling.

For any business, marketing first implies three things:

- It is a *concept*; the belief that the customer is of prime importance in business, that success comes from customer orientation, seeing the business through the eyes of the customer and producing what they want in the way in which they want it.

- It is a *function*; to define it formally, 'the management process that is responsible for identifying, anticipating and satisfying customer requirements profitably'. This must clearly be directed at senior level and take a broad view of the business. More simply put, someone must wear the marketing 'hat'.

- It is a *range of techniques*; not just selling or advertising (for which it sometimes becomes a smart euphemism) but all those techniques concerned – implementing marketing in all its aspects, market research, product development, pricing and all the 'presentational' and promotional techniques including selling, merchandising, direct mail, public relations, sales promotions, advertising and so on.

The first of these, which implies consumer orientation, sounds like common sense, and indeed is. However, this was not always the case, and a word about the history of the marketing approach may put matters in perspective. Looking back some years three clear stages can be recognised:

Production orientation (1945– late 1950s)

Supply and choice were limited. An organisation's major task in seeking profit was to pursue efficiency in production and distribution, because demand outstripped supply.

Sales orientation (the 1960s)

As competition increased, an organisation's main task in seeking profit was to stimulate the interest of potential customers in existing products and services; with demand and supply broadly matched.

Marketing orientation (the 1970s onwards)

With demand outstripped by supply, and choice proliferating, the organisation's main task is to determine the needs and wants of target markets, and to satisfy them through the design, communication, pricing and delivery of appropriate and viable products or services – in the face of competitive activity (and all aspects of competitiveness seem set to continue to intensify).

This is illustrated graphically in Figure 1.1.

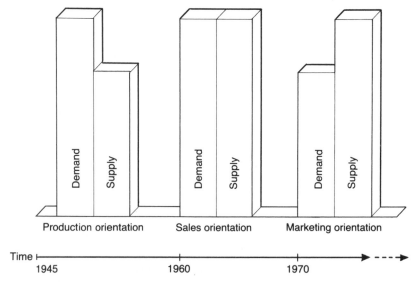

Fig. 1.1 History of the marketing approach

Now all this may well start to make things clearer, but it is still not the complete picture; marketing has to operate as a *system* and involves variables inside and outside the marketing organisation. The system links the market (customers and potential customers) with the company, and attempts to reconcile the conflict between the two. A moment's thought will show that the objectives of company and customer are not the same. For example, the company may want to sell its products for a high profit, whereas the customer wants the best value for money.

There are four elements that comprise the *marketing system* and these deserve individual review:

1 The market and its segments
2 The company and its various functions
3 The marketing mix
4 The external environment

We will look at these in turn.

3

The market and its segments

There is seldom a mass market for any product, though some companies presume that mass-marketing and advertising methods will successfully exploit such a mass market. Analysis has shown, however, that within each market there are actually a number of market segments, and this is true not only for common products which would be expected to have a 'mass market', such as breakfast cereals, butter and basic clothing, but also for more 'individual' products such as components and equipment, and for services such as hotels or plant hire.

Each segment represents a group of actual or potential customers with the same need which can be satisfied with similar products. For example, within one market for cars there are segments interested particularly in economy, status, or carrying capacity etc; and with detergents there are segments interested in softness (for the hands and clothes), cleaning power, economy etc. In industrial markets the same applies. Similar medical equipment sold to private clinics and to 'charity' hospitals in the Third World may perform the same function, but will have a different degree of sophistication for each segment, and each segment of the market develops a degree of buyer loyalty which can range from total loyalty to total indifference. Instead of mass-marketing, therefore, these segments often have to be tackled selectively and individually in order to achieve maximum profitability and the least conflict over the image of the company and its product.

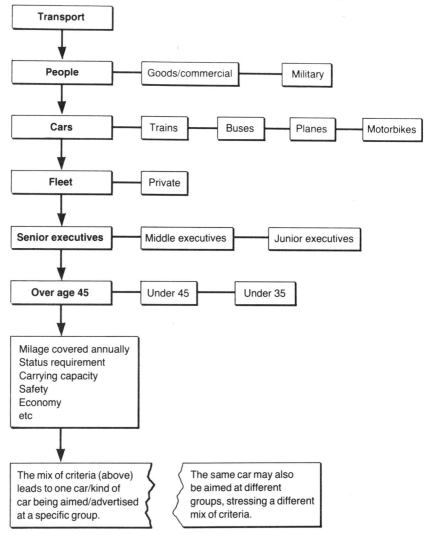

Fig. 1.2 Segmentation 'cascade' transport

Segments are not something a company invents, they have to be discovered, accurately identified, and then exploited individually. The example in Figure 1.2 shows how even a simplified version of a technique sometimes called a 'cascade analysis', demonstrates the many segments within what otherwise can be regarded as one, general, market area.

It is important that such a cascade is taken down to its lowest level; *quantifying* each segment can follow later, at which time such questions as, 'Is it desirable?' and 'Is it accessible?' can be answered. The lower down a cascade that a segment is identified, the higher will be the likelihood that the needs profile with be homogeneous (see Table 1.1). This kind of analysis can be applied, on a practical basis, to the thinking involved in marketing planning.

Table 1.1 Characteristics of a segment

Homogeneous	All consumers in the segment share the same *needs* profile
Desirable	It is sufficiently large to offer adequate opportunity for the fulfilment of corporate product objectives
Accessible	The segment can be reached cost and time effectively
Measurable	Its potential can be quantified and qualified

The company and its function

Every company has three basic functions, though in a well-directed company they do not operate in isolation from each other, and two major resources. The three basic functions are:

- **Production**
- **Finance**
- **Marketing**

The two major resources are:

- **Capital**
- **Labour**

Each function has different tasks and different objectives, often operates on a different time-scale, attracts different types of people, and regards money in a different way. So, despite their all contributing towards the same company objectives, there is inevitably internal conflict between, say, marketing and production, or production and finance.

The first boxed section entitled 'Implications around the company', further explores this conflict and how it can affect companies and the people in them. Perhaps you are yourself in a position where you are sometimes conscious of this, or where your department is pig-in-the-middle between two others.

Table 1.2 How conflict arises between different company functions

	Finance	Production	Marketing
Objective	To ensure that the return on capital employed will provide security, growth and yield	To optimise cost/output relationships	To maximise profitable sales in the market place
Time period of operation	Largely past – analysing results plus some forecasting	Largely present – keeping production going particularly in 3-shift working	Largely future – because of lead time in reacting to market place
Orientation	Largely inward – concerned with internal results of company	Largely inward – concerned with factory facilities for personnel	Largely outward – concerned with customers, distribution and competition
Attitudes to money	Largely 'debit and credit' – once money spent, it is gone, money not spent is saved	Largely 'cost effective' – hence value analysis, value analysis techniques and cost cutting	Largely 'return on investment' – money 'invested' in promotion to provide 'return' in sales and profits
Personality	Often introverted: lengthy training: makes decisions on financially quantifiable grounds	Usually qualified in quantitative discipline; makes decisions on input/ output basis	Often extroverted; often educationally unqualified; has to make some decisions totally qualitatively

IMPLICATIONS AROUND THE COMPANY (1)

Fact and friction

How does all this affect you, and others around the organisation? Well, you may have noticed that in most companies sometimes everyone does not pull together; there are conflicting pressures and conflicting objectives that make what individuals, and individual departments are trying to do more difficult. Why does this occur? There may be all sorts of reasons, but one is inherent. Every function within the company – production, finance and marketing being the main functions – actually has different objectives and different tasks to carry out. In addition, they operate on differing time scales, attract different types of people and regard money in different ways. So, despite being part of an organisation working towards common objectives, there is inevitably some internal conflict between, say, marketing and production, or production and finance. Table 1.2, though to some extent a caricature, shows clearly how this sort of conflict and friction occurs.

Understanding this, and learning enough about the different aims another person or department has is the first step to reducing unnecessary friction.

7

The marketing mix

This describes 'the offering' of the company to the market, and consists of three elements:

- **The product range**
- **Prices**, discounts and terms
- **Presentation**, or means of communicating with the market (selling, sales promotion, advertising etc.)

Juggling with these three elements enables a company to balance its objectives with the consumers' objectives.

The effect of technological development and the vigorous competition that exists in a capitalist society has resulted in products and prices of competing companies in most industries becoming increasingly similar. Consequently the first two elements of the marketing mix are becoming less important to customer choice, and presentation (the way in which the company tells the market about products and prices) has become crucial. Often it is the only differentiating element between companies.

Presentation includes all communication techniques including advertising, promotion, direct mail, personal selling, merchandising, packaging, and display and service (now often referred to as customer care). All these have to create an image, and a difference in perception, both by emphasising real product differences and/or adding something extra. The extra element may well be intangible, but this does not make it any less real. For instance, all watches tell the time, and these days usually do so accurately. But some sell primarily on fashion considerations (Swatch) or status (Rolex). The fact that there is rarely one simple factor but a multitude of interlinking ones makes for greater complexity. Watches, to continue the example, are bought for many reasons – many as presents – selecting a particular model may involve consideration of price, design, status, fashion, brand image, features (does it tell you the date, or the phases of the moon?) and many more. The ranking of these factors will be different to a degree for different people.

All this may make it sound as if marketing people can elect to exert influence as and where they want. Not so, as the next section shows.

The environment

This whole marketing system has to operate in an environment which restricts it. Such restrictions include:

1 Total demand
2 Availability of capital and labour
3 Competition (including international competition)
4 Legal requirements
5 Supply of raw materials
6 Channels of distribution – e.g. overseas agents and conditions

Any restrictions must be carefully considered, because of their effect on the business. For instance, competition is easy to recognise as a restriction. Few companies are monopolies (and if they are many governments will try to stop that situation continuing – or starting, in the case of mergers), but what is competition? Other companies making and selling the same product? Yes, but it is more than this.

Take an example – a book, perhaps a novel or travel book rather than a business book such as this. Who is the publisher competing with? Other publishers of similar books are only the beginning. Competition is broad. The publisher is selling a product that fills leisure time, so is in competition with the theatre, records, movies, television and video, magazines and newspapers. Developments in these areas affect his market. For example, how much has the advent of in-flight movies reduced the number of books passengers read and thus sales at airport bookshops?

But competition is broader still; book purchase comes from discretionary income, it is in fact not essential (or so, as a regular book buyer, I am always told at home!). So competition comes also from other products entirely, the socks or pullover that need replacing perhaps. Expenditure is even reduced in a month when there is a particularly high telephone bill in the home of a regular book buyer.

In addition, many books are given as presents, so items with a similar price which may also make attractive or appropriate gifts also feature as competition; pens, ties, costume jewellery and so on. Restriction means just that. Some factors are at least bound up with the business and comparatively easy to work with. The lack of an overseas distributor in, say, Malaysia may hamper a firm's export, but it is easily recognisable and action can, potentially, be taken to correct the situation.

Other factors are truly external, and some act long rather than short term. All can have direct impact on markets and marketing opportunities – for good or ill. Consider a classic historic market change. In 1979, in the UK the market for large motorbikes (those with engines over 250cc) was considerable and growing – with

9

Japanese manufacturers predominating. Three years later the number sold had dropped to less than a quarter of the previous number. Why?

- **Socially** – fashions changed (it was the first 'yuppie' period) and it became less socially acceptable to be a 'biker'.
- **Politically** – the law changed making it more difficult and time consuming to obtain a licence to ride a large bike.
- **Technically** – the increasing technological sophistication of large bikes, particularly in their use of electronics, made home servicing and maintenance only possible for the most proficient and dedicated owners.
- **Economically** – the inclusion of the more sophisticated elements, inevitably necessitated raising buying prices (almost, in some cases, to the level of a small car).

10

It was the combined effect of all these factors which caused a major shift in the market. If such changes are not recognised, or worse still, not anticipated and acted on, then damage will be done; and, if competitors react more quickly or more effectively, then a company can be left behind.

Watching the signs in all these areas may also create opportunities, as the following examples illustrate:

- **Social** – demographic trends (an ageing population in the UK), or lifestyle changes affect markets for products linked to, say, diets, holidays and health.
- **Political** – regulations on safety affect both product design and price.
- **Technically** – a technological development like fax has created new product opportunities worldwide (and no doubt reduced the market for post and telex).
- **Economic** – reduced taxes affect price and thus demand, major economic developments such as are occurring as the European Economic Community reshapes itself can create new export markets.

So, what does marketing do to achieve its aims and lead the company through the potential minefield of external factors that may influence it? It undertakes the continuous implementation of the **marketing process** (yes, *another* use of the word). This cycle of activity is shown in Figure 1.3, and starts, not surprisingly, with the customer. As the process goes on we can see how some of the classic marketing activities feature and how they relate to the concept in carrying out their specific role.

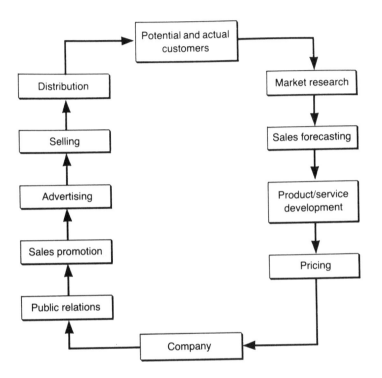

Fig. 1.3 The marketing process

First, **market research** attempts to help identify, indeed anticipate consumer needs; what people want, how they want it supplied, and whether they want it differently in the future. As research can analyse the past and review current attitudes, but not predict the future, it must concentrate on trends and needs careful interpretation. Next, **forecasting** must be used to try to ascertain how much of a product/service may be purchased in future. Identifying a clear need is of little use commercially if only a handful of people want it.

Product and/or service development is a continuous process. Sometimes the process is more evolution than revolution as a product gradually changes, sometimes it is more cosmetic than real (a new improved floor cleaner with ingredient X), sometimes it is so rapid consumers get upset by the pace of obsolescence – as in computers where you know that if you have the latest model, it must be obsolete. *Price* mentioned earlier is a marketing variable; price says a great deal about quality and must be set carefully, not only to ensure financial objectives are met, but to create the appropriate image in the market place.

EXTERNAL COMMUNICATION

With these factors in place, the company must *promote* itself; that is communicate, clearly and persuasively to tell people what is available and encourage them to buy. A variety of techniques can then be used, together or separately (these are reviewed in Chapter 4). Of all the promotional tactics, selling (reviewed in Chapter 5) is the only personal one, involving one to one com-munication, and it often forms a last important link in the chain of different methods that link the company to the market. Lastly, an important part of marketing is **distribution.** Marketing some-times involves a direct relationship: you see an advertisement in the newspaper and reply direct to the company, who send you the product. More often there is a chain of intermediaries. Where did you obtain this book? – possibly direct from the publisher, but more likely from a bookshop. If so, the publisher may have sold it to a wholesaler who in turn sold it to a bookshop. Similarly, the new brake light bulb you buy for your car may go from the manufacturer to wholesaler to garage to you; other chains may be longer (more of this in Chapter 6).

This process or cycle of marketing continues all the time, and already some of the different facets of marketing are falling into place. As we will see it involves as much art as science; it is a creative process which has some scientific basis, but no guarantee of success. The customer is always fickle and unpredictable; marketing may be an exciting function of business, but it carries a real element of risk.

Summary

So, marketing is much more than simply a department – or a body of techniques; it is central to the whole reason for a company's being and to its relationship with its market and its customers. While, of course, many activities of a company are important, a commercial organisation can only create profits out in the market, so unless marketing creates a situation where customers buy sufficient product (or service) at the right price and at the right time, the operation will not be commercially viable. Marketing has to produce in customers a reason to buy, and a more powerful one than any competitor produces; whatever the many elements involved, the key is to focus on customer needs and set out to satisfy them at a profit.

13

IMPLICATIONS: Review and Action	
Your Job	Related Areas
POINTS TO REVIEW	POINTS TO REVIEW
POINTS TO ACTION	POINTS TO ACTION

14

2

The foundation of marketing planning
The Cheshire Cat's advice

Every management guru there has ever been has plundered, wittingly or unwittingly, Lewis Carroll's writing in *Alice in Wonderland* and come up with a maxim along the lines of 'if you don't know where you're going, any road will do'. The original, from the moment when Alice meets the Cheshire Cat at a crossroads, puts it with considerably more elegance and style:

> 'Would you tell me, please, which way I ought to walk from here?'
> 'That depends a good deal on where you want to get to', said the Cat.
> 'I don't much care where . . .' said Alice.
> 'Then it doesn't matter which way you walk', said the Cat.
> 'So long as I get *somewhere*', Alice added, as an explanation.
> 'Oh, you're sure to do that', said the Cat, 'if you only walk long enough.'
>
> *Alice's Adventures in Wonderland*, Lewis Carroll

However it is said, it is good advice. Every company needs clear objectives. If these are too simple, they are less than helpful in a practical sense. The Managing Director who says only that 'our objective is to make as much profit as possible', is merely stating a self-fulfilling prophesy. To be useful a plan must be in writing and have a degree of formality. There are three main reasons for this, and all relate to the fact that the plan should not only set out *what* will be done, but *how* it will be achieved. They are:

- First to be certain that all the objectives set by the firm are clearly related to specific actions (and by corollary that large amounts of expensive time are not taken up by activities which have little or no effect on the achievement of objectives).

- Secondly, that the individual efforts of all staff are concentrated on the actions specified by management. In particular, all staff should be aware of the *key priority* actions which keep the firm in business today and tomorrow. At its simplest, these could include ensuring that every customer account is examined to identify additional business potential, or perhaps that invoices are submitted immediately they are due.

- Thirdly, that all the activities specified in the plan can be measured, assessed and improved, as the planned year progresses.

Now it is not the purpose of this chapter to set out guidelines as to exactly how to write a marketing plan, rather it is to air some of the issues inherent in the process. The starting point is the key objective from which strategic planning can flow.

The key objective

It is not true to say that America leads in everything, though they are seen as the originators of much marketing thinking, but they certainly lead in one area – the creation of new jargon. Not so long ago the phrase *mission statement* came into the language. Like it or not, it is descriptive of a clear statement of the purpose and key objective of an organisation. And such a statement is useful to both thinking and communication (and subsequent attitudes throughout an organisation).

Too often it is believed that a company's mission is obvious or 'goes without saying'. However, it may be obvious only to top management without it permeating the organisation to generate *shared company values* and style. Many businesses pay only lip service to the need for a company mission by publishing a meaningless motherhood-type statement such as: 'Our goal is to satisfy customers and make a profit'.

A properly constructed mission statement, one which considers the many dimensions of a company's relationships with its stakeholders, and which includes time, purpose and direction, should be the definitive statement of why the company is in business, how it intends to remain in business and with what resources the business will be managed.

When management senses that the organisation is drifting, or new opportunities become available, it must renew its search for purpose. It is time to ask some fundamental questions:

- What is our business?
- Who is the customer?
- What represents value to the customer?
- What will our business be?

These apparently simple questions are among the most difficult a company will ever have to answer. Successful companies continuously raise these questions and answer them thoughtfully and thoroughly.

The mission of an organisation is shaped out of five key elements.

The first is **the history of the organisation**. Every organisation has a history of aims, policies and accomplishments. In reaching for a new purpose, the organisation must honour the salient characteristics of its past. It would not make sense for Harrods, for example, to become a discount store even if such a move reflected a growth opportunity.

The second consideration is **the current preferences of the management and owners**. Those who direct the company have their personal goals and visions.

Third, **environmental considerations** influence the purpose of the organisation. The environment defines the main opportunities and threats that must be taken into account. The Girl Guides would not attract new recruits in today's environment were it to continue pursuing an earlier mission statement: 'To prepare young girls for motherhood and wifely duties'.

Fourth, **the organisation's resources** make certain missions possible and others not. Virgin Airlines would be deluding itself if it adopted the mission to become the world's largest airline.

Finally, **the organisation should base its choice of purpose on its distinctive competences.** McDonald's could probably enter the solar energy business, but that would not be making use of its main competence – providing low-cost food and fast service to large groups of customers.

A mission statement should also specify the business domain (or market) in which the organisation will operate. The business domain can be defined in terms of three dimensions:

- the customer groups that will be served
- the customer needs that will be met
- the technology that will satisfy these needs

In almost all cases *market definitions* of a business are superior to product definitions of a business. A business must be viewed as a customer-satisfying process, not a goods-producing process. Products are transient, while basic needs and customer groups endure forever.

Turning the mission into concrete goals and objectives facilitates the process of market planning, implementation and control.

Such a view may change progressively but is useful; it not only needs keeping up to date but, in the longer term, as it is thought through, can affect the whole direction of the business. An example is perhaps the best way to make this clear.

Company X were a scaffolding firm, a traditional business; asked what business they were in, they would originally have replied – seeing it no doubt as self-evident – 'scaffolding for the building industry'. True enough, though by its nature a current or historic description and a somewhat limiting one.

Looking ahead, and searching for markets beyond building, it was discovered that other areas of construction (as varied as chemical plants and North Sea oil rigs) needed scaffolding. The description shifted to 'scaffolding for the construction industry', and the organisation changed to take advantage of these additional opportunities.

So far so good, but what really was it they sold? Discussion defined this as 'temporary access and support', now a little way from the original description of the business, and this led to further searches for market opportunities and inroads being made with the leisure industry where large amounts of scaffolding are now used in contexts such as temporary spectator stands at everything from pop concerts to sporting events.

Seeking to take this thinking still further, and finding that technically their systems (joints, fixing etc.) were little different from competitors', they concluded that they did have an edge in the skill with which they were able to erect and dismantle their scaffolding, in terms of speed and safety. While the company had never seen export markets as a possibility (steel tube is prohibitively expensive to transport overseas), expertise can be exported. This, after further work (it is not being suggested that these kinds of shift are achieved without time, effort and investment), led to good business being developed in training others (for instance in the Middle East) to erect and dismantle to the same high standards.

The change wrought by this kind of thinking is clear, but it draws attention to another factor. It is easy to say, as in the case above, 'it was discovered . . .' but *how* is this kind of information brought to light? In a word, *research*, another important marketing technique.

Market research

There is more to research than the lady with the clipboard, by whom you may sometimes have been stopped in the street. Not only is market research an area with its own techniques and technicalities, it has to relate to overall marketing activity, particularly in planning and decision making. To help define terms, and make clear purpose, the following is quoted from the book *The Effective Use of Market Research* (Kogan Page, 2nd edition, 1992) written by Robin Birn, with whom I have worked in association regularly over some years and who runs Strategy, Research and Action Ltd. It is an excellent reference – now in paperback – for anyone who wants to know more in this area.

Decision making is central to carrying out managerial functions to make the planning and monitoring process work. Good decisions are taken on the basis of availability and use of relevant information. The information of most concern to marketing management comes from markets and customers, present, potential and future, and concerns the shape, size, nature, needs, opportunities and threats within the market. Market research is the means of providing them with that information.

Definition of market research

The traditional definition of market research is:

'The systematic problem analysis, model-building and fact-finding for the purpose of improved decision-making and control in the marketing of goods and services.'

This implies that research is not just an information tool but a means of providing guidance to help improve the abilities of management within an organization, as well as a means of making a contribution to the management of the marketing mix. It can be used to help decide on: the marketing strategy required to meet the challenge of new opportunities; which market gaps to approach; and which are the key areas of interest for future marketing strategies.

Purposes of market research

The two basic purposes of research are:

- to reduce uncertainty when plans are being made, whether these relate to the marketing operation as a whole or to individual components of the marketing mix such as advertising or sales promotion.
- to monitor performance after the plans have been put into operation. In fact, the monitoring role has two specific functions: it helps to control the execution of the company's operational plan and it makes a substantial contribution to long-term strategic planning.

Simply stated, research covers all the 'finding out' activities of marketing. It is the essential first stage of a marketing function – the identification of consumer needs. It covers five major types of research.

- **Market research** – who buys what in what quantity?
- **Product research** – what is right and wrong with the products of the company, or part of them
- **Marketing method research** – are we communicating and distributing effectively?
- **Motivational research** – why people buy the products they do and what they feel about them
- **Attitude surveys** – customers' attitudes to the products and to the companies who make them

Like any other form of research, marketing research can only investigate past behaviour. This is of course very helpful in predicting future behaviour but research as such cannot be conducted on the future. When attempts are made (opinion polling, intention surveys etc.) then serious errors can be made.

The role of research, therefore, is to improve the fact basis on which forecasts and decisions are made. The difference between researching the past and predicting the future must be clearly recognised.

SOURCES OF INFORMATION

- **Internal records** – a prime source which when processed can reveal much about the characteristics of customers, what they buy and how
- **Published information** – from whatever source
- **Field survey** – should only be used when the first two sources are exhausted, or surveys will be conducted which simply discover (very expensively) what is already known

TECHNIQUES OF RESEARCH

- **Sampling** – in most markets, to contain the research within practical limits sampling must be used. This uses probability theory to predict the characteristics of a total universe from a small section within definable limits. The commonest sampling methods are random and quota, particularly the latter as it is cheaper to implement

- **The questionnaire** – this must be carefully designed to ensure the forming of the questions does not bias the answer
- **Research methods** – questionnaires can be administered in person, on the telephone, or by post. There is an inverse correlation between accuracy and cost. In certain types of research, e.g. motivational studies, group interviews are often used

RUNNING A RESEARCH PROJECT

Management must first decide as precisely as possible what it wishes to know. To ask for 'everything about the market' is very expensive and often unusable.

Secondly, it must be decided whether to use internal staff (either researchers or other personnel, e.g. the sales force) or an outside agency. When the costs and possible prejudices of internal staff are considered, it is often at least equally economic to use specialists.

The project brief and method must be clearly defined and acceptable tolerances and timings set. If outsiders are being used, several proposals should be sought to ensure the fullest possible exploration of the problem.

When the findings are available, they should be checked against any other data and an action programme of decisions drawn up based on the facts identified. Otherwise, although very interesting, the survey will become yet another item clogging the filing system.

CONCLUSION

For research to give the value it should, management must define:

- What decisions do we have to make?
- When?
- On what information will they be based?
- How accurate does the information need to be?
- How quickly do we need it?

No company can risk operating without research, even though the 'research' is purely deep experience of company staff. As decisions get bigger, however, it is worth the insurance of real research to establish a better fact basis.

To conclude I will quote Robin Birn again (*The Effective Use of Market Research*) who describes the results of using research as a 'win-win' situation, and defines it so neatly it seems unfair to paraphrase the thought. The case that follows, taken from the same source, ends this section on a note which emphasises the practical contribution research can make to marketing and to marketing planning.

23

Using research is a 'win-win' situation for those who interpret it and action it effectively. Management 'wins' first time when the research confirms its prejudices, ideas and experiences so providing reassurances that it is taking the right decisions. It 'wins' a second time if the research provides new information or gives a new focus or emphasis on the subject being researched.

Over a period of time users of research also find that they 'win' a third time. If they take a step back to look at the original findings of the research objectively then they can design more interesting and more relevant research than had been completed originally. Research therefore helps management to 'win' by indicating the action it needs to take.

Case study – reappraising the results

This case study involves a packaging company whose main product base was the manufacture of high quality printed cartons and boxes. The company had recently invested in the most modern production plant, capable of producing superior quality products at lower costs and with a reduced turn-around compared to their competitors. Once the plant was in operation, it was realized that the necessary production volumes were not being achieved from the sales orders to make the plant viable. So the company decided to carry out market research with its existing and potential customers, to establish its market profile before deciding how to develop a strategy to obtain an increase in market share.

In-depth interviews were carried out with the major purchasers in the market to establish their attitudes towards the leading suppliers of packaging in terms of price, delivery, quality and general company image. Each individual supplier was rated in these terms against the other suppliers. The original packaging company had believed that the results would show the company to be amongst the leaders in quality and delivery performance, but average in terms of price.

The market research results, however, were not as expected. In fact, the results suggested that the company was bottom of the league on all factors except quality. In addition, it showed that the company had an overall image of being a "slow reacting company", only to be used for special work not required quickly and where price was not important.

These results obviously surprised the company and did not provide the answer to how to increase the volume throughput and the commercial viability of the production plant. As the results were being considered by management, certain more positive features became apparent.

First, they realized that the quality image was favourable and that it was a major reason why the company had the image of being a specialist work supplier. Secondly, the comments on poor delivery had been those associated with the company before its investment programme, and the buyers interviewed were not necessarily aware of the new plant and production facilities. Lastly, the perception of specialist work did not link with pricing, which was considered unimportant in this area.

Clearly the company's initial marketing strategy of being a high volume, low cost and quality producer was at variance with the market's image. It was also apparent from the results that a more significant market niche was available. Since its image was specialist, and once the message of increased volume with rapid delivery could be passed into the market, it would be possible for the company to increase its market share. More importantly, as this type of work was not price sensitive, higher profits could be made without direct comparison to competitive suppliers.

Here we have seen that the expected results of the market research were not obtained and the company's initial marketing approach appeared to be failing. As a result of the market research, intuitive analysis of the outcome showed that a definite marketing approach was possible which could provide greater success than had initially been targeted in the marketing plan. The market research gave the company much more actionable results than had been thought possible in the initial marketing planning.

IMPLICATIONS AROUND THE COMPANY (2)

Open Wide

Any pharmaceutical product is necessarily subject to many tests before it can be marketed to the public (a complex process which in most countries is regulated by government). The last stage consists of 'clinical trials'; that is doctors use the product with a limited number of patients and report back to the producer.

In one company they were launching a new product, a gel to treat mouth ulcers, and had reached the stage of such clinical trials. Information was slow to come in and the marketing manager became concerned about the effect on the subsequent schedules and launch date. His secretary, aware of this, thought about it and had an idea. It seemed so obvious that, for a while, not wishing to appear stupid in suggesting something which had been thought of and rejected for good reason, she said nothing. But, as the delay became worse she plucked up courage. 'Surely', she said, 'the people who would hear about patients with mouth ulcers are not doctors, they're dentists'. Eureka! they had *not* thought of it (all previous products had clearly been for prescription by doctors), the test was restarted with a panel of dentists and, in due course, the launch proceeded on time.

Moral: many aspects of the marketing process need ideas, and most marketing people do not care who has them, they just need sufficient to keep the process working effectively. In the kind of circumstances described above, the worst that could have happened would be for the idea to be inappropriate; while it could not then have been used, the interest taken would no doubt have been applauded. The situation is always wide open, the next idea might be one that matters.

Compiling the plan

This is a task that may involve a number of people, from the Managing Director down (*see* Table 2.1) but must be co-ordinated by the senior marketing person and contributed to by others. You may like to consider, as you study Table 2.1, who is involved in your company.

Table 2.1 Contributors to the marketing plan

Planning	Job function (your company)	Responsibilities
Purpose and direction of all business activities.		Overall approval and control of organisation. Reports to top management.
Purpose and direction division (broad strategy and general resource allocation).		Approval and control of divisional performance.
Marketing and overall product portfolio information collected, analysed and projected.		Evaluation and assigning of priorities. Controls planning and implementation of approved plans.
Marketing and product information collected, analysed and projected. Determination of individual product strategies, tactical plans and control of progress.		Preparation of individual product plans. Monitoring of implementation co-ordination of product-related resources.
Management and direction to achieve company product sales targets.		Implements and provides feedback on divisional plans in the field.
Individual sales activities to achieve sales target.		Achievement of sales targets and related customer contacts.

Without getting bogged down in too much detail, and leaving the question of the variety of strategic options on one side (we pick this up in the next chapter), the main stages involved are as follows:

Stage 1 – Formulate overall direction and goal

These are answers to the question 'what business are we in?'

If the business is looked at in terms of customers, not products, a new orientation to the company can be developed. Needs and benefits, not functions or features, should be the focus. As the President of Revlon said: 'In the factory we make cosmetics but in the drug-store we sell hope'.

It is too easy to become myopic and see only what the company sells; the danger is that as market needs change they are not recognised.

27

Business definitions should be narrow enough to provide direction, yet broad enough to allow the growth and response to changing market needs. The most productive approach is to define a business in terms of the needs it can satisfy and the segments of the market it can service. Thus, in order to be able to satisfy a market need and through this make a profit, a company needs to look critically at itself and identify:

- Its strengths – what it is *good* at doing
- Its weaknesses – what it is *bad* at doing

The plans can then concentrate on:

- Exploiting, perpetuating or extending strengths
- Avoiding, minimising or eradicating weaknesses
- Converting weaknesses into strengths, e.g. by training

Stage 2 – Identify the external opportunities

The aim here is to determine the market potential for own products in terms of needs that are not being fully satisfied. The needs of all segments should be considered.

This stage of the process involves segmentation of the total market, and often indicates where market research should be directed.

Stage 3 – Identify the external threats

As well as identifying opportunities and threats from customers and prospects, it is also important to consider the threat to existing revenue and profit. This will come from competition, demand and other environmental factors.

This stage of the process involves collecting data, the making of assumptions and production of forecasts for the business.

Stage 4 – Analyse internal strengths and weaknesses to produce marketing objectives and strategies

The marketing planning process is concerned with how the resources available to the company can be used to exploit the opportunity.

Marketing goals must be realistic – this is achieved by analysing strengths and weaknesses and asking: 'Why should we be able to exploit the market opportunities we have identified?'

Generating strategies is essentially a creative task. Ideally, the more alternatives that are generated the better. A good strategy will identify the main lines of business activity which will remain constant over the total planning period and provide the framework for tactical decision-making. Strategy aims to answer the question: What basic activities should we carry out?

Stage 5 – Programme the marketing mix

Within the framework defined by the strategy this stage is concerned with determining the detailed programmes that attain the goals. The overall approach involves:

1 Breaking down the marketing mix into:
   – the product elements
   – the pricing elements
   – the promotion elements
2 Programming the activities of each.
3 Integrating the separate programmes of each into the marketing plan.

Stage 6 – Communication and control

The elements of the promotion are concerned with identifying and implementing the most appropriate communication activity between the company and its potential customers. It integrates the activities of personal selling with those of non-personal selling: advertising, PR, sales promotion and merchandising, and concerns decisions on the methods and types of sales effort required.

29

Once the plan has been approved it can be distributed. The final format of the plan must be such as to encourage revisions before senior management confirms its adoption. Controls consist of bringing actual and desired results closer together. It is a four stage process:

1 setting standards
2 collecting information
3 variance analysis
4 corrective action

Clearly, more people than the marketing manager and his immediate staff will be involved in the creation of a marketing plan.

An analysis of (probable) participants and their roles was shown in Table 2.1, on page 26.

Note: stages 2 to 4 are what is often referred to in discussions of planning as SWOTs analysis (that is strengths, weaknesses, opportunities and threats; the internal and external considerations). Such considerations are, of course, specific to any individual organisation. Figure 2.1 shows an example, summarising this view of a medium-sized accountancy firm.

Fig. 2.1   An example of SWOTs analysis

EXAMPLE Firm's strengths and weaknesses

1 Client base
1.1 What is our current client base, by size, by location, by industry?
1.2 How does our disposition of clients (client mix) compare with the market mix?
1.3 Are our clients in growth sectors of the market?
1.4 How dependent are we on our largest clients?

2 Range of services
2.1 How closely does our range of services reflect the market's needs?
2.2 How does our range compare with competitors?
2.3 Are the majority of our services in growth or decline?
2.4 Is our range of services too narrow to satisfy our markets?
2.5 Is our range too broad to allow satisfactory management of performance?

3 Fee structure
3.1 What is the basis of our fee structure?
3.2 Do our direct and indirect competitors structure in the same way?
3.3 Are our fees competitive?
3.4 Do our clients perceive fees as 'value for money'?

4 Promotional and selling activities
4.1 With which clients/recommenders/influencers are we communicating?
4.2 What do they know and feel about the firm?
4.3 Are we communicating with enough of the 'right' people?
4.4 What means of communication are we using?
4.5 What attitudes exist in the firm towards 'selling' services?
4.6 Is each person in contact with clients capable of selling the full range of services?
4.7 Do they possess the necessary knowledge and skill in selling?

5 Planning marketing activity
5.1 Do we have agreed plans for the marketing and selling activity?
5.2 Do the plans state activities as well as objectives and budgets?
5.3 Do we have individual as well as corporate plans?

6 Organising for marketing
6.1 How is the firm's marketing activity organised and co-ordinated?
6.2 Are authority and responsibility for each person clearly defined?
6.3 Are our people committed to marketing the firm and its services?

---

7 Control and measurement of marketing

7.1 Have we defined 'success' for ourselves and our staff?

7.2 Have we established key result areas to measure that success?

7.3 Do these standards examine marketing as well as professional standards?

7.4 Do we measure performance against desired standards and take corrective action?

EXAMPLE Market opportunities and threats

1 How is the market structured quantitatively?

1.1 How many people/organisations of what type are there in our market who have a need for our kind of services (e.g. corporate/private/large/small/geographic location)?

1.2 What services do they currently use?

1.3 How much of the services do they use (e.g. annual spend)?

1.4 How often do they use the services (e.g. annually/monthly)?

1.5 Who do they use?

1.6 What services do they not use?

1.7 How do existing and potential users gain access to services like ours (e.g. personal recommendation/directories)?

2 How is the market structured qualitatively?

2.1 Why do existing and potential customers buy/not buy?

2.2 What do they think of the services they buy (e.g. good value/overpriced)?

2.3 What do they think of the firms who supply the services (e.g. too big/too small/helpful/unhelpful)?

3 How is the market served competitively?

3.1 Who are our direct competitors (i.e. other similar firms)?

3.2 Who are our indirect competitors (i.e. 'overlapping' firms)?

3.3 What are their strengths and weaknesses (e.g. services/size/staff/image/fees/marketing skills/geographic coverage)?

4 What are the quantitative and qualitative trends?

- market/segment size;
- market/segment requirements;
- market/segment structure;
- market/segment location;
- competition.

Summary

There is an old saying 'plan the work and work the plan'; it is good advice. Marketing planning is not an academic exercise, nor should it create a straight jacket which stifles flexibility or, still worse, creativity. What it is more akin to is a route map; it sets out the broad intention, and does so in sufficient detail to prompt the action appropriate to achieving objectives, but it also helps along the way. It makes possible prompt fine-tuning where necessary, not only to take corrective action if targets are not being met, but to allow advantage to be taken of additional opportunities met during the year.

In many ways marketing planning only forms the basis for three key questions:

- Where are we now?
- Where do we want to go?
- How will we get there?

and sets the scene for a fourth to be answered – how will we know when we get there? (A topic picked up in Chapter 7).

Finally, Figure 2.2 summarises the elements that should be, manageably, documented in the plan.

Fig. 2.2 Essential elements in the marketing plan

- A statement of assumptions made about economic, technological, social and political developments (both short and longer term).
- A review of the sales/profit results of the company (by product, market and geographic break down) in the previous period.
- An analysis of external opportunities and threats.
- An analysis of internal strengths and weaknesses (and comparative statements about competition).
- A statement of long term objectives (specific to growth, financial return etc.) and how they will be achieved.
- Next year's specific objectives.
- A plan of timed marketing activity, showing what will be done, in what order, and allowing co-ordination of the different elements.
- A link with intended outline plans for subsequent years.
- Comment on priorities of action linked to opportunities.

IMPLICATIONS: Review and Action

Your Job	Related Areas
POINTS TO REVIEW	POINTS TO REVIEW
POINTS TO ACTION	POINTS TO ACTION

In a position to succeed

Strategic approaches to the market

The plan, and the marketing planning process, referred to in the previous chapter poses a number of options, indeed, given free range the variety of options, at a number of levels, may be considerable. Yet only one course can be pursued at a time, at least in a particular marketing situation, and those in charge have to make, sometimes hard, decisions.

We will look at this by reviewing in turn three levels of decision making:

- The definition of *our market* (the group of customers/potential customers with whom the organisation hopes, or rather intends, to do business)
- The setting of clear *objectives* (desired results in the chosen market place)
- The selection of *strategic direction* (the course of action that is intended to achieve that result)

The market

The plan must recognise that a definition of market, indeed the market which a company believes it serves, is often difficult. *Too narrow a definition and a company's alternative strategies can be limited, perhaps disastrously. Too wide a definition and a company's strategies and resources can be diluted across too many competing opportunities.*

The problem is that the concept of 'market' has many interpretations. A market may be, for example:

- A group of people sharing a common interest (car drivers; computer-buffs; vicars; training managers)
- A particular part of the world (Milton Keynes; Granada TV area; the Middle East; the Southern sales region; the EEC; South East Asia)
- A broad business sector
- A narrow business sector
- A particular area of need that cuts across many market segments

Deciding what market a company is in (or should be in) is crucial to the objectivity – the focussing of – the corporate plan, and importantly, of the company's marketing, product management and pricing policies.

Having identified the market segments in which it is competing, a company has to assess how its products, their presentation and their packaging match the needs profiles of those segments. In doing so, the company has to recognise it has the choice of four broad market types:

Undifferentiated markets
As the name suggests, this approach provides a blanket, take-it-or-leave-it marketing package that covers just about everyone likely to buy. This strategy (which ignores the fact that consumers make choices and enjoy doing so) can be dangerous, because it leaves a firm open to attack by competitors attempting to seize sub-segments by appealing more closely to very specific segment needs.

Concentrated markets
This attempts to closely match services or products with the needs of a narrow market segment.

Being a big fish in a small pool has many advantages, especially for smaller firms lacking the resources to compete in much broader or multi-markets.

This specialist kind of service has its disadvantages too. If there is a business downturn in that narrow segment, the company may lack a sufficiently broad base of alternative buyers to whom resources can be quickly re-directed.

Differentiated markets

Broadly, this represents a compromise between the above two extremes. This marketing approach looks at the entire range of segments within a particular market and seeks to satisfy those of sufficient size and potential reward with precisely targeted but very similar products. (For example, Volvo Penta manufacturers diesel engines for pleasure craft. Within that closely defined market it has a model for every significant segment from outboard motors to 50 metre luxury cruisers.)

Served markets

This is a term which implies little purposeful planning, for served markets are the markets which a company presently serves, whether or not there is advantage in so doing. In other words, market opportunities have led the company into sectors perhaps in an unco-ordinated manner, rather than the company devising a co-ordinated strategy to take it into the most advantageous sectors. Such companies are said to be 'opportunity-led' rather than 'strategy-driven'.

37

With a clear view of the market it is aiming at, the company can turn to setting objectives.

Marketing objectives

Clear objectives exist to focus and to place any tactical activities in order of priority. Clear, means quantified wherever possible (rather than all-embracing statements: 'we will aim to make as much money as possible'). A nmemonic illustrates whether this has been achieved; objectives should be SMART, that is:

S – Specific
M – Measurable
A – Achievable
R – Realistic
T – Timed

DEVELOPING MARKET STRATEGIES

Beyond that the overall *objectives* available must be considered. There are, in fact, surprisingly few, perhaps six main ones, shown here followed by some possible *strategies* for achieving them:

- *To increase the share of the existing market* (necessarily winning business from competition) – through: concentration on selected segments; developing product applications; using different brand names.

- *To expand existing markets* – through: increasing frequency of customer purchase; increasing usage; opening new branches.

- *To develop new markets for existing products/services* – through: approaching new market segments; export marketing.

- *To develop new products/services for existing markets* – through: revision of old products; introduction of radically new things.

- *To develop new products/services in new markets* – through: diversification; takeover; technological extension.

- *To increase profitability of existing business* – through: improving value offered to customers; marketing audit and productivity improvement; reduction of range.

Such options are not, of course, mutually exclusive. Often a combination can provide even stronger effect in marketing plans. However, the greatest danger for a firm, at the point of selecting appropriate strategies, is that it may be tempted to adopt too many courses of action. Such a mistake spreads management too thinly and prevents commitment of maximum effort to the prime and most important courses of action.

Marketing planning, then, must begin with a thorough and creative attempt to choose the most appropriate focus for the entire firm's marketing effort.

Whichever route is chosen it is best reviewed against a checklist to see that:

38

- It satisfies the needs of the various precise target groups at which it is aimed – consumers, wholesalers, customers, etc.
- It achieves the corporate marketing, financial and growth objectives.
- It gives direction to various elements of marketing activity – products, prices, distribution, promotion.
- It blends well with other strategies, i.e. does not hinder their achievement.
- It capitalises on the corporate strengths and minimises the effect of any weaknesses.
- It gives competitive advantage which is difficult to match or surpass.
- It is within the competence and resources of the company.

Where to aim

39

At the same time decisions must be made about 'positioning' – the place selected within the range of options represented by the market. For example, Ford and Porsche both make cars, but, although Ford make some higher performance and quality cars, they would be seen as somewhat down-market from Porsche. The two are 'positioned' differently from each other in the market; something incidentally that is separate from their size, profitability or other measures that might be made of them.

The nature of a product is usually considered to be the most important element of the total marketing mix. Based on the marketing objectives and strategies of a company, management must make a variety of decisions on product mix, product lines, brands and services. These decisions are critical to the continuing prosperity of the company and it is therefore important to assess fully, *relative to competition*, how well products perform in terms of *the needs they aim to satisfy* and development programmes.

In evaluating product performance it must be recognised that products are bought for what they do rather than what they are; that the benefits conferred by a product are created not only from its actual physical features, but also from a whole constellation of other objective and subjective characteristics such as availability, reputation, after-sales service, and more.

In many markets, especially but not exclusively the consumer ones (referred to sometimes as FMCG – fast-moving consumer goods, such as soap, coffee and washing powder) the *brand*, that is the product name, is crucial in terms of what is called *brand image*. This is the product and all that goes with it. So, the brand image of, say, an airline includes everything from the service, the fares, the livery, check-in arrangements, as well as behind-the-scenes elements such as maintenance and safety procedures, to the name and the way it is all presented in promotion and advertising. The kind of brand image that will be created needs deciding on. Sometimes this is wide, designed in effect to be all things to all people; sometimes it is very narrow – what is called 'niche marketing' – and directed at smaller focussed segments.

40

Note: probably the ultimate classic piece of marketing jargon is U.S.P., standing for unique sales proposition. This is what makes one product, or brand, different – or seem different – from another. It is an amalgam of the actual characteristics of a product, its design, features, and, perhaps above all, image.

Also, primarily in consumer markets, the cost of launching a new product is considerable (and the failure rate is high too, with only 1 in 10 new products surviving any length of time – a further demonstration of the fickle nature of the market). This means that often the first launch uses a *test market*. Instead of launching nationally, it is tried out just in a smaller region, a county or Independent TV region (if TV advertising is to be used). This may reduce the risk, but even then there are key considerations to be taken into account:

- *When to launch the product:* If the product is replacing an existing one, should the stocks of the old product be run down? If demand is seasonal and the season is well advanced, should the launch be postponed until next season?

- *Where to launch the product:* It is important to choose an area where rapid acceptance and payback can be achieved rather than launching it in the stronghold of a competitor.

- *To whom to launch the product*: Often, certain sections of the population are more open to new ideas than others and so are willing to try it. These should be the first segment targeted.

- *How to launch your product:* A clear promotion strategy needs to be planned to get PR, advertising and selling to reinforce each other and produce optimum results.

Product life cycle

No product goes on for ever. Some are here today and gone tomorrow, as with fashion products, a pop record or a newspaper or magazine. Research shows that whether the life is short or long the pattern is similar, taking the form of a bell-shaped curve, usually divided into five stages known as:

41

- Introduction
- Growth
- Maturity
- Decline
- Phase out

Introduction is a period of slow growth as the product is introduced in the market. The profit curve shows profits as almost non-existent in this stage because of the heavy expenses of product introduction.

Growth is a period of rapid market acceptance and substantial profit improvement.

Maturity is a period of slowdown in sales growth because the product has achieved acceptance by most of the potential buyers. Profits peak in this period and start to decline because of increased marketing outlays to sustain the product's position against competition.

Decline is the period when sales continue a strong downward drift and profits erode toward the zero point.

Finally, **Phase out** is the period when the product is withdrawn.

The designation of the beginning and end of each stage is somewhat arbitrary. Usually, the stages are based on where the rate of sales growth or decline tends to become pronounced.

Not all products pass through the idealised bell-shaped product life cycle. Some products show a rapid growth from the very beginning, thus skipping the slow sales start implied by the introductory stage. Other products, instead of going through a rapid growth stage, go directly from introduction to maturity. Some products move from maturity to a second period of rapid growth.

Support for the product life cycle concept lies in the way innovations are usually adopted into a marketplace. When a new product appears, steps must be taken by the company to stimulate *awareness, interest, trial*, and *purchase*.

This can take time, and in the introductory stage only a few persons ('innovators') may buy it. If the product is good, larger numbers of buyers ('early adopters') are drawn in. The entry of competitors into the market speeds up the adoption process by increasing the market's awareness and by exerting a downward pressure on prices.

More buyers come in ('early majority') as the product is legitimised. Eventually the rate of growth decreases as the proportion of potential new buyers approaches zero. Sales become steady at the replacement purchase rate. Eventually they decline as (newer products) appear and divert the interest of the buyers from the existing product.

Thus the product life cycle is closely related to normal developments that can be expected in the diffusion and adoption of any new product. Figure 3.1 summarises all this graphically.

Think of a few well known products. Some have been around a very long time – Bovril, Persil, Cadbury's Milk Tray. Some maintain themselves through modification, effectively starting the cycle again at its peak; others remain very much the same for long periods, for example, Black Magic chocolates were launched in the 1930s and did not change a single flavour for some 50 years. Others go into the doldrums, sometimes for years, but are revived

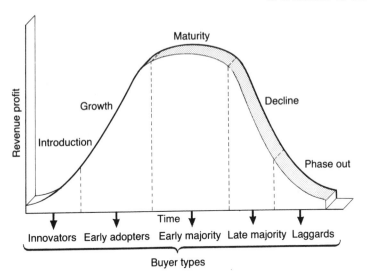

Fig. 3.1 Product life-cycle

43

like Brylcream, Hovis and Lucozade; still others disappear without trace, forever. All are evidence of the product life cycle, and the more long lived are usually a sign of successful marketing. You can doubtless think of more.

How much?

Every product has a price. The problem is deciding what it should be; it not only affects profit – clearly – it affects image. The word that goes most easily with cheap is nasty, yet everyone wants a bargain or, as a bargain is essentially something worth more than it costs (and therefore rare), what they want is *value for money*.

Price puts out many messages. It can say something is classy, good quality, fashionable, or shoddy. There is an apocryphal story that one of the first astronauts to go to the moon was asked what he thought about in the last few seconds of the historic countdown. He thought for a moment and said, 'I remembered that there were 5,000,000 working parts in the machine underneath me, and that, in every case, the contract had gone to the lowest bidder'. There are situations where low price does not boost confidence. Who wants the cheapest insurance, stockbroker or (if you go private) surgeon?

Price has other psychological impacts. For example, all the research shows that if a price is just below a round figure, £9.99 or £19.99, rather than £10 or £20, people will buy more. Probably no one really understands why, but many manufacturers and retailers use the fact and price accordingly. (The other reason this is done is for security – at such prices the shop assistant must give change, and thus must open the cash till and record the sale. Sadly, staff pilferage is a significant cost to be avoided.)

Similarly, the thinking about discount levels or retailers or wholesalers, quantity terms and so on all have to take account of the way people think about the figures. The use of price at annual or seasonal retail sales is another example. Of course, everyone wants to save money, but just how it is put is significant. Which sounds best on a £100 item, '½ price' or 'save £50' and, if it was reduced to £55, how different do 'almost HALF PRICE' or 'nearly £50 SAVED' sound?

So pricing policy is a vital part of the marketing peoples' jobs. And it is not a once and for all decision 'we will charge this much, and put it up by a percentage for inflation each year'; price can be, and is, used tactically, to steal an edge on competition. As an example of rather sneaky tactical pricing, one petrol station took business from a rival not 100 yards away, because as an independent they could make instant decisions, whereas the rival who was part of a major chain had to refer to head office through a system that took a whole week.

So, how are prices set? There are four basic approaches to pricing:

- Cost-based pricing
- Market demand-based pricing
- Competition-based pricing
- Market-based pricing

It is well worth determining price levels in a way that combines all four approaches.

COST-BASED PRICING (ACCOUNTANTS' APPROACH)

This is the approach similar to the way an accountant would calculate the price for a product. It is based on total cost of product, including production and marketing costs, plus an allocation for overheads plus the target percentage to provide a profit margin. The total gives a selling price.

Problems

- Cost calculation is based on a predetermined level of demand and production. As these fluctuate, so does the product cost.
- It ignores market factors such as demand and competitors' actions.
- Overhead cost allocation can lead to a wrong pricing decision

A major benefit of this approach is that it can help indicate *minimum* price levels.

45

MARKET DEMAND-BASED PRICING (ECONOMISTS' APPROACH)

The aim of this approach is to explore the effect that different prices may have on the demand in the market for a product. Here the marketeer will try to calculate the break-even point (produced by varying volume forecasts) based on different selling prices. This approach brings into focus the impact of price on volume and tries to find the most profitable price/volume ratio. They must ask themselves how many units of a given product they could sell at different price levels.

The *advantage* of the market demand approach is that it brings together price calculations with market demand realities; that is, if demand for a product tends to be a function of its price, then this should be a determining factor in the decision.

The *disadvantage* is the difficulty of estimating the effect that price variations may have on product demand: one has to estimate how much one can sell in units for a given price level. Given this problem, an easy way to establish price elasticity is to examine the historical performance of similar products at a number of different price levels to study the effect on sales of price.

COMPETITION-BASED PRICING

The objective of this pricing approach is that it considers the prices set by competitors in the market place. Competitive pricing can be approached in a number of ways:

- Prices can be set *above* competitors' products
- Prices can be set *below* competitors' products
- Prices can be set at the same level as competitors

MARKET-BASED PRICING

In this approach prices are based upon the 'value satisfaction' the product delivers to the buyer of the 'perceived' value. This 'perceived' value can be a result of:

- Value for money influenced by all aspects of the firm, and its product and service.
- Image affected by status (endorsement by opinion leaders, exclusivity or promotion).
- Reflection of different and distinctive market segment putting different 'value' on a product performance.
- Price barriers apparent in different segments.

The key to market pricing is to make an accurate assessment of a market's perception of the value of the product. Market research may be needed to avoid two dangers:

- Over-pricing because of an inflated view of the value of your product. Almost inevitably the 'perceived price' will be a qualitative judgement made by the buyer relative to his experience of the competition.
- Underestimating the real value and charging less than is possible.

PRICING STRATEGIES

Given a price range, a decision has to be made as to where in that range to locate a product's price. This is a strategic decision made on the basis of corporate and company objectives, which may include some or all of the following:

- Achieve target return on investment or sales
- Stabilise prices
- Maintain or improve market share
- Meet or prevent competition
- Maximise profits

Among the important approaches to price are:

Skimming price policy

This strategy sets a price at the top of the acceptable price range.

Advantages

- Used on a new product in early stage of life-cycle to recoup high investment
- To segment the market
- To prevent pricing mistakes by being too low – it is easier to reduce than to increase prices if wrong price level chosen
- To limit off-take if plan capacity or stocks not adequate

Disadvantages

- Attracts competition
- Low volume may not suit production
- Consumer awareness and acceptance will be slower in the introductory product life stage for a new product
- More vulnerable to economic depression

47

Penetration price policy

This strategy is the opposite of skimming. A low price is set, often below existing range with the objective to gain maximum market penetration as quickly as possible; that is, low price, high volume.

Advantages

- Product economy of large-scale production
- Pre-empts competition
- Wins wide product allegiance for future

Disadvantages

- Profit return is lower and pay-back period longer for a new product
- It will be disastrous if the product has a very short life-cycle
- It can be difficult to overcome the psychological disadvantages of having to increase price if the initial price was set too low

Marginal cost pricing

In highly competitive situations one may have the opportunity of gaining business if a sufficiently low price is offered. The question arises, however: what is the lowest price to use at which it makes sense to take the business? One approach is to use marginal costing which is defined as 'the cost of producing one more unit'.

The cost of producing one more unit means that the fixed costs are already being covered by the existing sales volume, and then the costs of producing the extra unit are the variable costs. If a small profit is made per unit, then at least this is an additional contribution which would not have been there had we not obtained the extra business. It can be argued that, even at no profit, marginal business is worth having as it may use resources that would otherwise stand idle. Generating this type of business, however, will ultimately eat into profits and depress the percentage of return on sales. The major use of marginal costing, therefore, is to answer the question 'Should I accept this order?' rather than as a pricing tool. This type of strategy is more often used with price elastic, high-volume products, where it is important to keep the sales volume up.

PRICING GUIDELINES

A few guidelines might be useful in summarising this important area of marketing.

- Pricing is not seen by the purchaser simply in terms of 'what is the cheapest', but rather as one element in the 'bundle of benefits'; that is, what the image of the product is in the mind of the consumer/user and hence the perceived value.
- Customers never buy on price alone. Yet too many salesmen will often argue that it is the sole purchasing motivator.
- Before you comment on competitive pricing strategies or price structure, make sure you have hard facts to work on. Otherwise you may well make pricing recommendations that are unnecessary or wrong.
- There is always a tendency to overreact in the face of what is seen as competitive price pressure. *Remember that brand leaders are rarely the cheapest. They are frequently amongst the most expensive.*

49

Finally, pricing is of fundamental importance. It is an important, creative aspect of the marketing job. The marketing plan should include actual prices, costs and margins at various levels (i.e. the pricing structure).

Prices of major competitor products should also be included along with recommended prices for each year of your marketing plan, shown as actual prices and percentage change for each distribution (wholesaler, retailer etc.) for each year. A brief statement of the pricing strategy and of the various pricing considerations must also be given to summarise the options and decisions. Figure 3.2 summarises the price setting process.

C

Fig. 3.2 Six steps to price-setting

First, the company carefully establishes its marketing objective(s), such as survival, current profit maximisation, market-share leadership, or product-quality leadership.

Second, the company determines the demand schedule which shows the probable quantity purchased per period at alternative price levels. The more inelastic the demand, the higher the company can set its price.

Third, the company estimates how its costs vary at different output levels and with different levels of accumulated production experience.

Fourth, the company examines competitors' prices as a basis for positioning its own price.

Fifth, the company selects one of the following pricing methods: cost-plus pricing, break-even analysis and a target-profit pricing, perceived-value pricing, going-rate pricing, or tender pricing.

Sixth, the company selects its final price, expressing it in the most effective psychological way; checking that it conforms to company pricing policies, and making sure it will prevail with distributors and dealers, the company's sales force, competitors, suppliers, and government.

Companies can then apply a variety of price modification strategies to the basic price (i.e. market skimming or market penetration strategies).

IMPLICATIONS AROUND THE COMPANY (3)

A visible percentage

A company selling industrial components gave their sales representatives considerable authority. They were true 'territory managers' and made many decisions relating to the customers on their patch, including matters relating to price and discount. This worked well, but, over time they developed a tendency to give away too much in higher discounts, perhaps more concerned to preserve their good relations with customers than with the company's profitability.

As the worry became known, someone in the office came up with an idea – a simple 'discount calculator', two revolving discs (normally used for conversions such as gallons to litres) which showed at a glance how many additional sales a representative would have to make to recover revenue lost by giving differing rates of discount. Figure 3.3 illustrates this.

The usefulness was not so much the calculation (any pocket calculator could work out that, say, for a given margin a discount of 10 per cent meant 40 per cent more product had to be sold to produce the same profit), but it acted as a visual aid, a reminder. And indeed, in the period after this was introduced and issued to sales staff, discount rates were managed much more tightly.

Such an idea is by no means the perogative of the marketing staff; a little creative thinking by someone in the Accounts Department, already familiar with the figures and how they work, is all that is necessary here – plus reasonable communication between departments.

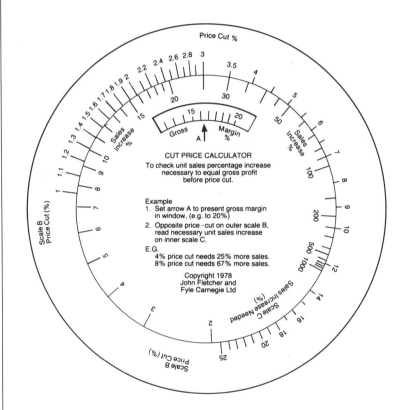

Fig. 3.3 Creative visual presentation of figures – a discount calculator for salesmen

Summary

There are, of course, products that do well in an enormous range of market positions. Some take the Rolls Royce view, others position themselves throughout the range of price and quality. There are many decisions to be made: design, price, image – everything that will give the product or service the greatest chance of success. Once a product is launched, the job of maintaining, and developing, initial success is a continuous one. There are larger issues too, especially for larger companies. Some make only one product (Wrigleys make nothing but chewing gum, but sell a very large amount, worldwide); others have a small, and sometimes tightly controlled range (it is only very recently that you could buy a cup of tea in McDonald's in *England*, even); others sell a wide, wide range of products, albeit organising themselves in a variety of divisions or separate companies to do so (like the 3M company who sell everything from materials for motorway signs, to office equipment and stationery); some launch endless new products (a major publisher could launch 30/40 new titles every month). All these decisions, and more, are ultimately judged in the market place, which is the only judge of commercial success.

However good all these decisions are, the world – or at least the chosen market – has to know about it. Promotion, the topic of the next chapter, is at the heart of marketing.

IMPLICATIONS: Review and Action	
Your Job	Related Areas
POINTS TO REVIEW	POINTS TO REVIEW
POINTS TO ACTION	POINTS TO ACTION

53

4

Telling the world
The promotional mix

This is, for many, the most interesting part of marketing; certainly it is the most visible, with elements of it – advertisements, posters and so on – all around us. It is also important, because as the well known 'better mousetrap' quotation at the beginning of this book makes clear, no business will be done even by the producer of the best product or service if no one knows of its existence.

Promotion is not, however, just a purveyor of information; it must be persuasive, it must differentiate. Remember potential customers may see the range of goods offered by competitors as somewhat similar. This is true of many areas, for example cars – consider how many very similar makes exist in each category – or fax machines. To a large extent it is the promotional elements that allow people to make a judgement about which is right for them.

Mix is the right word. The various promotional techniques are not mutually exclusive, they are often used together or in various combinations. Each works in a rather different way, principally in how directly it relates to the market. The diagrammatic view, Figure 4.1, shows the different distance at which each operates from the potential customer; it is this that characterises the different role which different techniques play.

Promotion does not act in a vacuum, it must relate to the way a potential purchaser moves progressively towards actual purchase, and act to change the attitudes of the target audience to

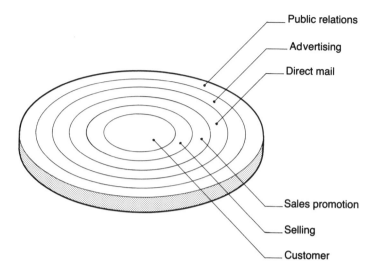

— Public relations
— Advertising
— Direct mail
— Sales promotion
— Selling
— Customer

Fig. 4.1 The communications mix

56

whom it is directed. With many products it is not just purchase that is the aim, but repeat purchase.

Diagrammatically the stages in the buying process are as follows:

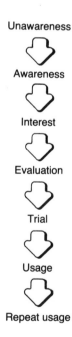

Unawareness

Awareness

Interest

Evaluation

Trial

Usage

Repeat usage

Each stage represents a tangible change and is worth examining sequentially.

Unawareness → Awareness

This is the stage during which a buyer moves from no knowledge of a product or situation towards a position where he knows about it. The buyer's attitude is nearly passive and his major need is to be informed. Promotion is targeted at:

- Telling the buyer that a product exists.
- Creating an automatic association between the needs area and the product.

Awareness → Interest

This is a movement from a passive stage to an active stage of attention. The buyer will have his curiosity aroused by the product's newness, appearance or concept. His response, however, can be conscious or subconscious. Promotional objectives are:

- To gain his attention through the 'message'.
- To create interest (motivation).
- To provide a succinct summary of the product (information).

Interest → Evaluation

The buyer will consider first the effect of the product upon his personal motivation (life-style, image, etc.). Then he will look at the effect on external factors. He will pass through a process of reasoning, analysing the arguments and looking for advantages. Depending upon his needs, he might look for improved efficiency or economy, uniqueness, reassurance or safety. Through promotion, an attempt is made to:

- Create a situation that encourages the buyer to start this phase of reasoning.
- Discover the buyer's relevant needs.
- Segment and target buyers according to the 'needs' requirements.

Evaluation → Trial

This is a key movement from a mental state of evaluation to a positive action of trial. The buyer's basic requirement is for a suitable opportunity to use the product. Promotional objectives are to:

- Clearly identify usage opportunities.
- Suggest usage when these opportunities occur.

Trial → Usage

The buyer will take this step if his trial has been successful. The objectives of the promotion are to:

- Provide reminders of key elements, such as brand, used areas, advantages, etc.
- Emphasise the success and satisfaction.
- Remind the buyer of usage opportunities and provide supporting proof via third-party references.

Usage → Repeat usage

This is the final objective for promotion. When a buyer moves from occasional usage to constant usage, he will have moved into a state where his selection of the product is automatic. The objectives are now simpler:

- To maintain the climate that has led to satisfaction.
- Maintain an acceptable image.
- Keep confirming the key qualities of the product.

With this in mind we can turn to and review how the separate individual techniques work, remembering that the effect they have is difficult to separate. A person's image of an organisation is the net and cumulative effect of everything they see and hear about it.

Public relations

Unless it is completely invisible, every organisation will have an image, but the question is whether it projects the right image. It helps to have a clear idea of how customers see a business at present. This is something that can be researched, but of course some information can be obtained by 'keeping one's ear to the ground', although remember, people will often say what they think is expected. Or worse, what is heard only confirms the existing view.

The effect of public relations (PR) is cumulative and a host of factors, perhaps individually seeming of no major significance, are therefore important. These include the quality of business cards and letter-heads, of switchboard and reception, of brochures, of staff appearance, and so on.

Consider any company you know of, one that has a strong image and of which you think well. Then think *why* this is so. Unless you have direct experience of them, it can only be because of what *they* tell you about themselves. Such messages can be powerful. Large companies will spend large amounts of money on their 'corporate image', something that hits the headlines occasionally (as with British Telecom a year or two back). But, large or small, the image matters. Everything from the overall logo (company symbol) to a one-man business's calling card.

Public relations must provide a planned, deliberate and sustained attempt to promote understanding between an organisation and its public. In fact, it must promote not just understanding, but a positive interest in the firm that whets appetites for more information, prompts enquiries, re-establishes dormant contacts and reinforces image with existing customers.

Not only is public relations activity potentially a powerful weapon in the promotional armoury, it is also free – well, at least compared with advertising, which is communication in bought space. But there is a catch. It takes time! And, perhaps particularly in any small business, time is certainly money. Therefore, in too many organisations public relations is neglected because staff

59

IMPLICATION AROUND THE COMPANY (4)

Nothing to do with me

Public relations links very much to a wide range of people in an organisation and to standards of service. Some well known fictitious examples occur in the award winning training film 'Who Killed the Sale?' (a film made by Rank — now Longman Training). The film shows a salesman trying, unsuccessfully, to get an order for some kind of engineering problem. Progressively, we see the potential customer exposed to others in the organisation and, cumulatively, such a poor image builds up that he is unwilling to place a new order — yet the salesman ends the film honestly wondering what went wrong.

A number of people are involved:

- A previous order is wrongly delivered, and the dispatch department, already at fault, makes matters worse by the poor way in which it attempts to sort it out.

- The switchboard operator contributes to an important message for the customer going astray when he visits the factory, as does a harassed girl in the sales office who fails to track him down.

- A demonstration is unconvincingly conducted by a technician who fails to realise its importance because he, in turn, was poorly briefed.

- A conversation is overheard by the customer, with two more technical people being dismissive about their own company's engineering competence.

And, the last straw, as the customer drives away from the factory he is held up, and made to reverse, by a rude delivery man who, when he closes his van door reveals the name of the same potential supplying company.

Such a list could be wider. Try thinking for a moment about your own company. What incidents can you remember? And can you list those people in a position to exert a positive influence on the process of building image — are you, perhaps, among them?

It takes few of these kinds of incidents to negate all the time and money spent on an expensive corporate image.

are busy, even over-stretched, and opportunities are missed. Yet if the power of public relations is consistently ignored, then at worst not only are opportunities missed but the image that occurs by default may actually damage business prospects. Certainly, for good or bad, many people are involved (*see* Implications Around the Company (4)).

In many ways, therefore, time spent on public relations is time well spent, and, while for smaller firms it can produce good low cost results, a larger firm able to sub-contract the activity to a PR agency may well spend substantial sums. If so, they will expect to see larger scale results, and much of that potentially comes through the press.

PRESS RELATIONS

Press relations is a very specific form of public relations that can pay dividends, although, unlike an advertisement, there is no guarantee of what is going to be said. Having said that, there is no reason to feel that the press will be critical.

Though personal contact with journalists and others is important, much can be achieved through the *press release*, a structured, written communication to the press intended to be the basis of a story of press mention.

Press releases can be in the form of routine mentions or more particular stories, but remember that much of the impact of both sorts of material is cumulative. Customers will sometimes comment that 'We seem to see mentions of the firm pretty regularly' but have difficulty remembering the exact context of what was said, or more likely written. To achieve this cumulative impact, the PR people need to be constantly on the look-out for opportunities of gaining a mention.

Even routine matters, perhaps the appointment of a new member of staff or a move of offices, may be written up and contribute to the whole process. It must all be thought of, done regularly, and done right. While some routine stories will get a mention, particularly if the company is well known, news means just what it says!

If marketing is so important why is it so few people understand it?

Marketing matters; but it can be confusing to the layman. Often used as a euphemism for advertising, or perhaps selling, it in fact encompasses a whole approach to business as well as a plethora of techniques to 'bring in the business'. And it *is* important; too important to leave to marketing people – many in an organisation are, wittingly or not, involved .

THE NEW BOOK:
MARKETING FOR NON–MARKETING MANAGERS by Patrick Forsyth is published in May 1993 and is intended to explain both the meaning and the importance of marketing.

Another book on marketing? Yes, but importantly *not* one aimed at marketing people. Published by Pitman Publishing in their new joint venture with the Institute of Management, it sets out to inform and demystify the marketing process. It not only shows the overall importance of marketing but also how it relates to many other parts of the organisation and the people in it.

The book covers the marketing concept, and how it operates as a function, a system and a process. It also discusses the various techniques involved from research to planning, from advertising and promotion to selling and distribution. It presents a practical, up to date view and makes clear the role of marketing in making an organisation successful and profitable.

The author, Patrick Forsyth, has written a number of other business books and is founding partner of Touchstone Training and Consultancy. He has worked in marketing consultancy and training for 20 years and is well qualified to explain the subject.

Publication date: **May 1993**

Price: **£14.95**

For further information or to request a review copy please contact Kate Salkilld on
071 379 7383

Press Release

Pitman Publishing, 128 Long Acre, London WC2E 9AN, UK. Tel: 071 379 7383 Fax: 071 240 5771

Fig. 4.2 Example of press release

While it may be of interest internally that the firm has 25 staff, inhabits an eighteenth-century mansion or is reorganising, a journalist will tend to find it difficult to imagine readers starry-eyed with excitement as they read it in their newspaper or journal. A company must find something with more of an element of news in it; it may be genuinely different, it may be a first comment on something, but it must truly have something of genuine interest about it.

If a company, or its spokesperson, becomes known as a source of good comment, stories and articles, then press contacts will start to come to *them*, and the whole process may gain continuity and momentum.

The press release that carries information of the type discussed here is a specialist document, which has to be put together just right – the detail of this is not important here, however an example may be useful. The example that follows, Figure 4.2, is the release planned on the publication of this book. Whether this will be picked up and quoted remains to be seen, but as an example of the kind of release that may generate comment it is reasonably typical.

63

Advertising

Next advertising, something we all see all around us day by day. First a definition: Advertising is '*any paid form of non-personal communication directed at target audiences through various media in order to present and promote products, services and ideas*'. More simply, it can be called '*salesmanship in print or film*'.

The role of advertising, as one of a number of variable elements in the communication mix, is '*to sell or assist the sale of the maximum amount of the product or service, for the minimum cost outlay*'.

There is a variety of forms of advertising, depending upon the role it is called upon to play among the other marketing techniques employed, in terms of both the type of advertising and the target to which it is directed.

These include, by way of example:

- National advertising
- Retail or local advertising
- Direct mail advertising
- Advertising to obtain leads for sales staff
- Trade advertising
- Industrial advertising.

A more specific way of understanding what advertising can do is to summarise some of the major purposes of advertising – that is, the objectives that can be achieved through using advertising in particular ways. A representative list, which is by no means comprehensive, is as follows:

- To inform potential customers of a new product/service
- To increase the frequency of use
- To increase the use of a product/service
- To increase the quantity purchased
- To increase the frequency of replacement
- To lengthen the buying season
- To present a promotional programme
- To bring a family of products together
- To turn a disadvantage into an advantage
- To attract a new generation of customers
- To support or influence a franchise dealer, agent or intermediary
- To reduce brand substitution by maintaining brand loyalty
- To make known the organisation behind the product/service (corporate image advertising)
- To stimulate enquiries
- To give reasons why wholesalers and retailers should stock or promote a product
- To provide technical information about a product/service.

There are clearly many reasons behind the advertising that you see around you. These are not mutually exclusive, of course, and many of those listed apply, or could apply, to your business. Whatever specific objectives the use of advertising seeks to achieve, the main purpose is usually to:

- gain the customer's attention;
- attract customer interest;
- create desire for the product or service; and
- prompt the customer to buy.

Advertising is, therefore, primarily concerned with attitudes and attitude change; creating favourable attributes towards a product or service should be an important part of the advertising effort. Fundamentally, however, advertising also aims to sell, usually with the minimum of delay, although perhaps a longer time period may be needed in the case of informative or corporate (image building) advertising.

65

Every advertisement should relate to the product or service, its market and potential market, and as a communicator it can perform a variety of tasks. It can:

- **Provide information:** This information can act as a reminder to current users or it can inform non-users of the product's existence.
- **Attempt to persuade:** It can attempt to persuade current users to purchase again, non-users to try the product for the first time and new users to change brands or suppliers.
- **Create cognitive dissonance:** This means advertising can help to create uncertainty about the ability of current suppliers to best satisfy a need. In this way, advertising can effectively persuade customers to try an alternative product or brand. (Extreme versions of this would appear to come under the heading 'knocking copy' – used sometimes by, among others, car manufacturers – which is openly critical of competition.)
- **Create reinforcement:** Advertising can compete with competitors' advertising, which itself aims to create dissonance, to reinforce the idea that current purchases best satisfy the customer's needs.

Moreover, advertising may aim to reduce the uncertainty felt by customers immediately following an important and valuable purchase, when they are debating whether or not they have made the correct choice.

Types of advertising

There are several basic types of advertising and these can be distinguished as follows:

Primary – This aims to stimulate basic demand for a particular product type – for example, insurance, tea or wool.

Selective – This aims to promote an individual brand name, such as a brand of toilet soap or washing powder, which is promoted without particular reference to the manufacturer's identity.

Product – This aims to promote a 'family' branded product or range of related brands where some account must be taken of the image and interrelationship of all products in the mix.

Institutional – This covers public relations-type advertising which, in very general terms, aims to promote the company name, corporate image and the company services.

And, of course, a variety of different media.

ADVERTISING MEDIA AND METHODS

There is a bewildering array of advertising media available. Here are some of the most popular methods of advertising, with a guide as to how they are used.

- **Daily newspapers** often enjoy reader loyalty and, hence, high credibility. Consequently, they are particularly useful for prestige and reminder advertising. As they are read hurriedly by many people, lengthy copy may be wasted.
- **Sunday newspapers** are read at a more leisurely pace and consequently greater detail can be included.
- **Colour supplements** are ideal for advertising, but appeal to a relatively limited audience.

- **Magazines** vary from quarterlies to weeklies and from very general, wide-coverage journals to very specialised interests. Similarly, different magazines of the same type (e.g. fashion) appeal to different age and socio-economic groups. Magazines are normally colourful and often read on a regular basis.

- **Local newspapers** are particularly useful for anything local, but are relatively expensive if used for a national campaign. They are sometimes used for test market area advertising support.

- **Television** is regarded as the best overall medium for achieving mass impact and creating an immediate or quick sales response. It is arguable whether or not the audience is captive or receptive; but the fact that TV is being used is often sufficient in itself to generate trade support. Television allows the product to be demonstrated, is useful in test marketing new products because of its regional nature, but is very expensive.

- **Outdoor advertising** lacks many of the attributes of press and television, but it is useful for reminder copy and a support role in a campaign. Strategically placed posters near to busy thoroughfares or at commuter stations can offer very effective, long-life support advertising.

- **Exhibitions** generate high impact at the time of the exhibition but, except for very specialised ones, their coverage of the potential market is low. They can, however, perform a useful long-term 'prestige' role.

- **Cinema**, with its escapist atmosphere, can have an enormous impact on its audience of predominantly young people; but without repetition (i.e. people visiting the cinema once every week) it has little lasting effect. It is again useful for backing press and television, but for certain products only, bearing in mind the audience and the atmosphere.

- **Commercial radio**, playing popular music for young people, offers repetition and has proved an excellent outlet for certain products. It is becoming apparent that the new local radio stations appeal to a wide cross-section of people and thus offer 'support' potential to a wide range of products.

Table 4.1 Choosing the appropriate media for your recruitment advertisement

Media	Advantages	Disadvantages
1. National dailies and weeklies	– large circulation – minimum delay before advertisement is published – proofs supplied to enable final advertisement to be changed or mistakes corrected – Specialist staff frequently available to give advice	– typesetting variable in paper-set advertisements – expensive – your advertisement competing with large number of others
2. Local daily, evening and weekly newspapers	– attracts local people and so avoids waste – costs lower than nationals – minimum delay before publication – acts as a guarantee back-up to a national advertisement at little cost	– would not be seen by good candidates outside circulation area – specialist jobs unlikely to draw sufficient number of applications – may not be seen by senior people
3. Trade specialist magazines	– usually inexpensive compared with national newspapers – seen by specialist readership if you are only intending to address this group, e.g. those in specialist industry	– long delays between each issue, frequently one month – advertisements often not seen by target audience for weeks after publication – job advertisements rarely featured prominently – not usually regarded by senior people as a primary source of jobs
4. Specialist selection agency publications of candidate lists (recruitment only)	– very cheap or free – large number of specialist categories to choose from – quantity available useful guideline to whether spending money on advertising will be worth while	– lists usually made up of professional job hunters/job hoppers – facts often suspect or, like estate agents' house descriptions, the truth is embroidered
5. Commercial radio and television	– very wide coverage especially at peak listening hours – speeds of acceptance of advertisement and broadcast – impact – more people listen to radio and watch television than read newspapers – gain attention of those not necessarily thinking of using/ changing accountants therefore less likely to notice advertisements in newspapers	– usually very expensive – cost usually means insufficient information can be provided – risk of not being seen or heard by those available during evening or at weekends

68

Not all these (or direct mail, reviewed later) are right for everything. Some are simply not cost-effective in certain circumstances; you are unlikely to see, say, an individual bookshop advertising on TV, but may well do in a local newspaper or on a poster in the shopping precinct. Every advertiser must make their own decisions (advertising agencies who handle the larger advertising budgets have sophisticated media buying departments), not only about different methods, but about exact media – one newspaper versus another and so on. Table 4.1 shows the comparative advantages and disadvantages of different media; this relates to recruitment advertising, something most managers look at from time to time.

Not all advertising, however, is aimed at potential consumers.

TRADE ADVERTISING

It is often not sufficient to advertise to consumers alone, particularly, where it is important that distributors/retailers are willing to stock and promote a product.

Even if the sales force has a prime role to play in ensuring that stocking and promotion objectives are achieved, trade advertising also has an important role to play in this respect:

- It can remind distributors about the product between sales visits.

- It can keep distributors fully informed and up to date on developments and changes of policy.

- It can also alleviate problems associated with the 'cold-call' selling of less well-known products.

Trade advertising is usually confined to specialist trade publications and the use of direct mail communications from the company to its distributors.

Most trade advertising occurs prior to major consumer advertising campaigns to help ensure the buying in of stock in anticipation of future demands to be created by the consumer advertising. Thus, when new products are launched, or special promotions introduced, trade support is often achieved through special offers ('13 for the price of 12') or increased (introductory) discounts, all of which trade advertising can effectively emphasise.

This type of advertising can also communicate to the trade the advantage of new products, as well as the timing and 'weight' of advertising support that is to come.

ADVERTISEMENT STRATEGY

Presupposing that the analysis of the market has led to a sensible choice of media and advertising strategies, then these have to be communicated to whoever is going to produce the advertisement. At its best, the advertisement strategy statement is brief and economical, and does its job in three paragraphs:

- The basic proposition – the promise to the customer, the statement of benefit, to whom.

- The 'reason why' or support proof justifying the proposition, the main purpose of which is to render the proposition as convincing as possible.

- The 'tone of voice' in which the message should be delivered – the image to be projected, and not infrequently the picture the customer has of himself/herself, which it could be unwise to disturb, or rather, wise to capitalise on.

In various fields some of the finest and most effective advertising has sometimes been produced without reference to an 'advertising strategy', or for that matter without knowledge of market facts. However, although research cannot always give all the details, or for that matter always be infallibly interpreted, it can give strong indications and reduce the chances of failure.

Most executives, when faced with a rough or initial visual and copy layout, have an automatic subjective response. 'I like it/I don't like it'. And while the creator may attempt to explain that the appraiser is not a member of the target audience, it is obviously difficult to be objective. Nevertheless, while an attempt at objectivity must be made, there are few experienced advertising or marketing executives who can say that their 'judgement' has never let them down. Advertising remains as much an art as science. (The most famous saying about advertising is that of the company Chairman who said 'I know half the money I spend on advertising is wasted, but I do not know which half' – a remark that contains a good deal of truth, and a sobering thought in light of the amount of money in some advertising budgets.)

Companies must ask straight questions about their advertising generally and about particular advertisements:

- Does the advertisement match the strategy laid down?
- Does the advertisement gain attention and create awareness?
- Is it likely to create interest and understanding of the advantages of a particular service?
- Does it create a desire for the benefits and conviction of the need to buy?
- Is it likely to prompt potential clients to action?

71

In other words: Does the advertising communicate? Will people notice it, understand it, believe it, remember it and buy it? Table 4.2 summarises the intention and thus 'shape' of a typical advertisement.

The next question is *how* can it be made creative? There are many

Table 4.2 Ingredients of good advertising

Objectives	Methods
Gain customer's attention	Select right media; buy enough space; impact headlines/pictures
Interest reader	Involve customer; make big promises; solve problem; present facts; communicate quality
Make reader desire benefits of your service	Show benefits for them; Don't bore – enthuse; testimonials; message clear and simple; be honest
Get action from reader – make a sale	Summarise benefits; ask reader to buy, call, telephone, attend reception, fill in coupon, make a choice, save time and money, buy now; ask for order

ways; humour, personalities, exotic locations, cartoons, even running advertisements in the form of a serial, ending with a cliff-hanger to encourage viewing the next. (Gold Blend coffee was the first to use this, at least in the UK, and even ran ads saying no more than the time and date of the 'next instalment').

In other words, advertising needs to be creative, often its task is to make something routine, or even dull, 'interestingly different'. Just occasionally the product really is interestingly different, more often the essential qualities of the product need presenting in whatever way allows the presentation to persuade. I described this in an earlier book (modestly titled *Everything you need to know about marketing*,* which took a light-hearted view of marketing activity) in a way which, while not entirely serious, does make clear the approaches involved and is worth quoting here:

Sometimes the product is such that with no competition, with a perfect match with customers' needs, all the advertisement has to do is say what the product will do for them.

'New instant petrol – one spoonful of our additive to one gallon of water produces petrol at 1p a gallon'. If your message is like this, no problem, persuasion is inherent in the message. But few products are like that. More likely any product will have competition, what is more it will be very like its competitors. Then you have to say more about it. Or start by thinking of everything about it. You may even say everything about it:

'SPLODGE – the big, wholesome, tasty, non-fattening, instant, easily prepared, chocolate pudding for the whole family.'

Or you stress one factor, thus implying that your competitors' products are lacking in this respect:

'SPLODGE – the easily prepared pudding.'

Customers may know all puddings of this sort are easy to prepare, but they are still likely to conclude yours are easiest. The trouble with this approach is that in a crowded market there are probably puddings being advertised already as 'easily prepared'. And big, wholesome and all the rest for that matter. What then? Well one way out is to pick another factor ignored by your competitors because it is not essential:

Everything you need to know about marketing, by Patrick Forsyth, is a Kogan Page paperback.

'SPLODGE – the pudding in the ring pull pack.'

It may be a marginal factor but your advertisement now implies it is important and that competition is lacking. Alternatively you can pick a characteristic of total irrelevance:

'SPLODGE – the pudding that floats in water.'

Or link it to the pictorial side of the advertisement:

'SPLODGE – the pudding you can eat on the top of a bus.'

If competition has done all of this then you have only one alternative, you must feature in the advertisement something else, nothing to do with the product. This may necessitate giving something away:

'SPLODGE – the only pudding sold with a *free* sink plunger.'

Or re-packaging:

'SPLODGE – the only pudding in the *transparent* ring pull pack.'

73

The possibilities are endless and the ultimate goal is always to make your product appear different and attractive, desirable because of it.

In addition, advertising has to be made to look attractive. Sometimes this may be achieved through the added humour, personalities and whatever, or through lavish production values – some television commercials cost far more per minute than many of the programmes they punctuate, and the photographic and editing values of something like Coca Cola's international advertising is clear to all. A danger here is that the pluses hide the message, viewers of a poster say, laugh at its humour but cannot recall what the brand name was on it.

Direct mail

Although direct mail is merely a particular form of advertising it is sufficiently important to merit a few words under its own heading. It is an important, and effective, media. Only the worst of it should be called 'junk mail', and some perhaps deserves it; as Samuel Johnson said, 'What is written without effort, is in general read without pleasure'.

Somehow feelings about direct mail seem to run high. Some people regard it as intrusive. Everyone appears to know someone who has been mailed three times in the same week about something entirely inappropriate, and addressed wrongly as 'Dear Madam'. Some people regard it as more than intrusive, ranking it somewhere between picking your teeth in public or being unkind to animals.

Direct mail is, in fact, only a form of advertising. No more, no less; albeit a specialised form. It is used very successfully in a wide range of industries and applications, many of them perfectly respectable – charities, banks, building societies and so on. Many others are dependent on it as their main form of promotion or because it results in a major proportion of their sales (indeed, one example of this is business books.) What is more, although of course there is the occasional annoyance, it is used for the most part without upsetting the people to whom it is directed. If they are not interested, they throw it away, a process which is not really so unlike turning over an advertisement page in a magazine in which one is not interested. Of course direct mail is wasteful. It hurts to think of so many carefully penned words ending up in the bin. (At least it hurts the originator!) But it is no more wasteful than other forms of advertising. All advertising is in a sense wasteful – what matters is whether it produces a cost-effective response, whether it pays for itself long term.

74

Contrary to popular belief, direct mail is read. In the UK, the Post Office, which spends a great deal of time and money studying the effectiveness of direct mail, recently demonstrated through research that more than 90 per cent of it is opened and more than 75 per cent of it is read. The trick is less to achieve this, therefore, than to ensure your offering will stand out from others, will generate interest and will be seen as persuasive.

Direct mail is not an alternative to advertising, rather it adds to the range of techniques available. It is no more a magic formula than any other individual technique. But it can sometimes suit well. It is flexible; certainly more flexible than advertising. Direct mail may mean either four letters, or 40, 400, 4,000 or 40,000. It does not have to be done on the grand scale, it can be targeted at small specific groups; it can be undertaken progressively with so many shots per week or month being sent. It is personal and can be directed at the decision makers, their advisers or both. It is controllable, it can be tested, implemented progressively and results can be monitored to ensure it provides a cost-effective element in the total promotional mix. As it is likely to be low cost per contract, and campaigns can be varied so much in size, there are likely to be very few organisations which could not experiment with the technique. It is specific and may be directed broadly, selling the firm, or be part of the promotion of particular.

So, direct mail has a lot going for it. It is a proven technique in many fields. It can be used on a small scale, it can be targeted on specific market segments, and it can be tested and monitored much more easily than many other forms of promotion. But, it is also deceptive and can appear easier to use than, in fact, it is. Every element of it needs careful consideration.

75

Among the components are:

- **The list.** Any mailing is only as good as the list. It must be appropriate, up to date and personal. Mailings addressed to an individual do best. In many businesses existing customers are as important as prospects, complex overlapping campaigns are constructed; there is a specialised area of 'data-base marketing' and, though list holding and use is now covered by the Data Protection Act in the UK, sources of lists are valuable. Next time you are asked in a store to write your name and address on the back of the cheque, that may be the reason.

- **The message** is vital, copywriting in this area is a specialist job. One phrase changed can increase (or decrease) the response. There are about three seconds, when something is pulled out of an envelope, in which the recipient decides whether or not to read on further.

- **The envelope** is part of the message, many are printed, perhaps with a 'teaser' message; what is on them affects response.

- **The letter** is vital and is often not short. A good message is as long as is necessary to present an argument to buy and if this takes four pages so be it; many letters are longer and work well.

- **Brochures** provide supporting information in a profusion of ways. They may be coloured, illustrated and, in extreme cases, incorporate a range of gimmicks from prize draws to stamps.

It is a technique where tiny details matter. For instance, a letter with a PS may do better than one without; a reply card with an actual postage stamp (rather than with prepaid postage) may get up to 50 per cent more replies; and certain so called 'magic' words (new, free, guaranteed, exciting) seem to boost response.

Look more carefully at the next 'shot' you receive. The best represent the 'high-tech' end of advertising, and while many talk of 'junk-mail', many more buy and buy again.

Sales promotion

In formal marketing terms, sales promotion can be defined as: 'An inducement aimed directly at persuading a specified target audience to achieve one or more defined objectives.' In simpler terms, it is a method of persuading people to take a course of action, which, without that persuasion, they would not normally take.

Sales promotion is an aid to selling, not a substitution for it. It is the tactic that is used because, after careful analysis of the facts and quantification of the objectives, it is likely to prove the most *cost-effective* method of meeting those objectives.

Sales promotion is not the answer if:

- All else looks doomed to failure
- The sales force has a period of inactivity
- Someone thinks it would be nice to have some
- The chairman's wife had a good idea

Yet, perhaps because it is an 'ideas' area, this is precisely what can happen. If the company tries to make a problem fit an idea, instead of creating a planned scheme to solve the problem, then experience shows that there is a very great chance that it will not work. Remember that, as with any area of promotion, if it is not precision *planned* and *controlled*, it could well have the directly opposite effect to the one it set out to achieve.

THE ROLE OF SALES PROMOTION IN MARKETING

Sales promotion is not an incidental that should only be used as a last minute afterthought; nor should it be left to area sales staff to plan and implement. It is an integral part of the marketing mix, and, as such, requires the same degree of planning as does the mounting of a market research project, or the selling-in of a new product. Effective planning is, therefore, essential, whether sales promotion is to be used as a support activity for the company's long-range objectives or as a short-term tactic.

77

A more specific way of understanding what sales promotion can do for the company is to summarise some of the major purposes of sales promotion, or the objectives that can be achieved through using it effectively in various ways, namely:

- To introduce new products, by motivating customers to try a new product or induce business customers to accept it for resale

- To attract new customers, by motivating existing customers to try a new product or induce business customers to accept it for resale

- To maintain competitiveness, by providing preferential discounts or special low prices to enable more competitive resale prices to be offered

- To increase sales in off-peak seasons, by encouraging consumption 'out of season'

- To increase trade stocks, by special monetary discounts or quantity purchasing allowances, in return for holding greater than 'normal' levels of stock

- To induce present customers to buy more, by competitions to encourage customers to think of more ways and more occasions for using the product.

Generally, then, sales promotion is a marketing device to stimulate or restimulate demand for a product during a particular period. It cannot overcome deficiencies in a product's style, quality, packaging, design or function, but can provide an important addition to advertising activities as an integral part of the communications mix.

We will now turn to some examples of what can be done. The list is no doubt not comprehensive as a new promotional idea is thought up somewhere every minute of the day. Indeed, there are no hard and fast rules for selecting the 'right' sales promotion tactic, since what is successful in achieving an objective in one industry may not necessarily be successful in achieving a similar objective in another. Similarly, the same promotion tactic might be suitable for meeting different objectives.

In practice, there are likely to be many alternatives, all of which would be suitable for meeting the same objective. Selection can be assisted by answering the following questions:

- Which promotion tactic best fits the profiles of the target audience?
- What are the advantages of each promotion tactic?
- What are the disadvantages of each promotion tactic?
- Which is likely to give the greatest level of success for the budget available?

The types of promotion tactic currently available are many and, while they cannot be strictly confined into set categories, the following list shows something of the range:

CONSUMER PROMOTIONS IN-HOME

In-home consumer promotions can help to pre-empt the attempts of competitors to solicit impulse purchases via in-store advertising and display. Techniques used here are:

- sampling, where a sample of the product is delivered free to consumers' homes, say;
- coupon offers via postal and door-to-door distribution, news-

paper or magazine distribution, and in-pack/on-pack distribution;

- competitions.

CONSUMER PROMOTIONS IN-STORE

Clearly, this type of promotion has the major advantage in that it is featured at the location where the *final* decision to purchase is made. Techniques used here include:

- temporary price reductions;
- extra value offers, including free samples banded on to normal and economy packs;
- premium offers (incentives), including free mail-in premiums, self-liquidating premiums and banded free gifts;
- point-of-sale product demonstrations;
- personality promotions.

79

IMMEDIATE CONSUMER BENEFIT PROMOTIONS

Here, consumer reward for purchasing is immediate, and, as with most incentives, the sooner the reward can be expected and received after the qualifying action, the greater will be the positive effects of that incentive in stimulating purchase action. Included in this promotion category are:

- price reductions;
- free gifts;
- banded pack offers;
- economy packs.

CONSUMER PROMOTIONS BY DISTRIBUTORS

These include the following:

- special trade-in prices for used goods;
- free gifts, such as an electric food mixer with a refrigerator;
- trading stamps or gift vouchers;
- mail-order promotions, such as special prices or credit terms.

TRADE PROMOTIONS

Reasons for promoting to the trade:

- to obtain support and co-operation in stocking and promoting products to customers;
- to induce distributors to increase their stock levels, where research may have revealed lower than average stockholdings;
- to pre-empt competitive selling activities by increasing trade stocks.

Techniques used in trade promotion:

Bonusing – this can take the form of monetary discounts or 'free goods' ('13 cases for the price of 12'), or special quantity rate terms.

Incentive schemes – These can be tailored to the needs of a distributor's sales force. Alternatively, annual, or promotional, sales targets may be set and agreed with distributors, and extra cash incentives paid according to the extent to which sales exceed the target. May also include competitions, particularly for sales staff.

Dealer loaders – Instead of money, gift incentives may be offered to distributors, or their salesforce, for achieving agreed sales targets or stocking certain quantities of product.

Thus, it can be seen that trade promotion can be an extremely important element within the total market strategy in helping to ensure that stocks are available in the right distribution channels and at the right time.

Co-operative advertising schemes – Assistance with preparation of advertisements or media costs.

Provision of display materials – Either free of charge or on a shared cost basis.

Tailor-made promotions – Custom designed to the outlet's individual requirements often promoting their own name and corporate image.

INDUSTRIAL PROMOTIONS

While sales promotion was pioneered in the consumer goods market where it is most visible, it is also used, albeit in slightly different ways, in industrial marketing. Reasons include the need:

- To encourage repeat purchase
- To secure marginal buyers
- To meet competition
- To ensure that bills are paid on time
- To stimulate a sales force or a dealer or agency network
- To induce rapid market penetration when launching a new product
- To sustain perception of value over and above that intrinsically possessed by the product itself
- To reduce the perceived risk involved in buying expensive and long-lasting items of equipment
- To smooth out costly buying cycles

81

If behaviour can be changed in these ways, to whatever extent, then the selling organisation will be more productive and profitable. Figure 4.3 shows some examples of the way things work in this area.

We will now investigate industrial promotion further in a way intended not only to show how this works, but to explain the differences inherent in this kind of marketing. Having said that, the approaches that follow can be applied more widely. Industrial products have been chosen to illustrate that not only are industrial promotions available (see previous section), but also that there is a practical way of combating industrial competition, other than through cutting price, and also a systematic approach to developing such promotions.

What distinguishes consumer from industrial goods firms is not only the nature of the product but, more importantly, its destination. Industrial goods are sold to other organisations (what is called 'derived demand'), and they are not always distinguish-

Fig. 4.3 Examples of industrial promotions

Price-off promotions: Special terms for specific customers at specific times.

Couponing: Coupons entitling the holder to special terms.

Competitions: Prizes awarded to sales staff or middlemen for achieving pre-set objectives.

Loyalty schemes: Give-away to loyal customers, £50 off next purchase

Reciprocal trading schemes: Guaranteeing to a customer that your organisation will in turn buy his product.

Credit schemes: Leasing, consignment schemes or delayed invoicing.

Premium offers: Special 'linked product' package deals ('13 for 12' offers) or free spares.

Trade-in allowances: Special terms for trading in a competitive or obsolete model.

Guarantees: Extra special guarantees for specific risky products.

Sampling: Distributing trial offers of a product, free demonstrations of trial installations.

Co-operative advertising: Allowance given for dealer advertising featuring a specific product.

Training schemes: Free training for operatives or middlemen.

Container premiums: Products distributed in a free multi-use container.

Full-range buying schemes: Special terms for across-the-range orders.

Co-operative promotions: Offering a range of products and services as a 'system' with the help of complementary suppliers.

able from consumer goods. Some, for example cars, typewriters, fuel, nuts and bolts, clothing, stationery, etc are sold to both.

Of course, at the other end of the size scale, the product differs substantially, but here it forms the minority of transactions, however important each one is individually. Having established the importance of the destination in categorising an industrial product, let us now look at the significance of that destination in determining the nature of the appropriate sales promotion. This can be illustrated by considering various situations and recognising that in practice there is often considerable interaction between them. Each situation, however, requires validation before it can be accepted as an accurate representation of industrial marketing situation.

The more discretion a buyer has over choice of product or supplier, the more his buying behaviour will approximate to that of the consumer.

The 'buyer' is a person who has most influence over the nature, size, direction and timing of an order, and may be a group of key people. In such a situation it becomes possible to transfer the use of promotional schemes, suitably modified in terms of content, to solve a particular industrial problem, straight across from consumer to industrial marketing.

The more discretion a buyer possesses, the more open he is likely to be to what can be termed 'idiosyncratic' as opposed to 'organisationally' directed buying behaviour. Factors that may affect the amount of discretion possessed by an industrial buyer are:

83

- Degree of power possessed (the more power, the more discretion)
- Length of time successfully served as the buyer
- Uniqueness of the contribution made to the firm's success
- Routineness of the task
- Organisational philosophy of the firm (given the level in the hierarchy at which an order is customarily placed; the more decentralised, the more discretion)
- Pressures on the need to buy

By considering criteria such as these, a company can completely reappraise its promotional approach, so as to take advantage of consumer goods techniques.

The larger the deal, up to a point, the more the appeals of the promotion should be aimed at increasing the monetary value of that deal, and at guaranteeing performance.

At very high order values, status, prestige, vagaries of high technology and politics begin to play a dominant part in the purchase decision. Orders can be swung by diplomatic pressure on, say, the chief executive or by the opportunity for reciprocal trading, for example. It is assumed, however, that between low and high value deals the 'economic' or 'budgetary motive' prevails for deciding the terms of the deal. As long as the customer organisation believes this to be true, and as long as it insists that buying decisions at middle value order levels are best made by several people, then the seller is forced to offer promotional schemes emphasising 'value for money', for example, cost reduction schemes, guaranteed delivery performance and quality control standards. Other schemes may be acceptable, but only if they legitimately help the buying group as a whole to achieve its objectives.

The more standardised the product and the more generalised the statements it is possible to make about the problems it solves in use, the more generalised can the promotional proposition be.

84

This is obviously logical, but it does illustrate how you can determine the 'precision' of promotional offers you make and, thus, for example, the best way of communicating them; for example, through the media or the sales force, to take two extremes.

The longer the time-span over which a buyer is committed to a product, the more promotions must be aimed at reducing perceived risk.

This is of paramount importance for products sold at the design stage (such as machine tools for the production line) perhaps years before commissioning or consumption.

Risks grow exponentially, especially in the buyer's mind, with the passage of time because of:

- Increasing difficulty of profit forecasting
- Technological risks of malperformance
- Obsolescence
- Misuse in the hands of inexperienced operatives and managers

These dangers can be alleviated by the imaginative use of promotional schemes, such as:

- Free consultancy, advice and training

- Guaranteed buy-back terms
- A financing or leasing scheme based upon revenue-earning capacity over time, rather than on a cost-incurring basis
- A suitably negotiated insurance deal to all customers at premiums lower than each one would obtain separately
- An effective technical and service back-up facility
- Trial installations

The more similar industrial products are to consumer goods, the more schemes, customarily used by consumer durable goods manufacturers, can be transferred to industrial markets.

The similarities are as follows:

- Similar purchase behaviour
- Both are often bought repeatedly, although the purchase interval can be longer for some
- Both are frequently sold through middlemen
- Both require financing, service, guarantee, insurance and linked package deals
- Both need special attention at their launching
- Both are sold through a sales force who themselves need motivation and support

85

In this way, and using these illustrative situations as a guide, any industrial organisation can begin to widen its effective choice of sales promotions, away from the rather overused and stilted panic price reduction, and based on adaptations from consumer goods promotions.

MERCHANDISING

It would be wrong to conclude this section on promotion without returning, primarily to consumer marketing, and reviewing briefly the area of merchandising. This is the term given to the promotional effect of how layout and display are arranged in retailers of all sorts. Have a look around you next time you go shopping. Are there shops with window displays that make you want to look inside? Do you notice, in a supermarket, that essentials, such as say bread or sugar, are always at the back of the store? This necessitates customers passing many other, less essential items en route to those they really want to buy. The word 'impulse buy' is used to describe purchases made on the spur of the moment because something catches the eye. This is not a way of making people buy something they do not want, so much as a way of making sure they buy sooner, rather than later and from somewhere else.

Merchandising and display have clear objectives and are designed to:

- **Sell more** that is to sell a quantity over and above the level that would occur if no action were taken. Some people will always want certain products and will search them out.

- **Inform** the customer about numbers of matters in numbers of ways; it tells them a shop is there, it indicates something of the range of products it sells, it highlights what is new, it directs people to the right section of the shop, and so on.
- **Persuade** making the message attractive, understandable and convincing – it is this aspect that can prompt the action that is really wanted; a sale!

It has to put over messages to many different groups of people. Perhaps particularly three:

- Those who may pass the shop by, who will not even enter unless something external catches their eye
- Those who come into the shop for one small item and who may buy more, and the ubiquitous 'browser' (a regular feature of bookshops, maybe this paragraph caught your eye as you did just that!)
- Those who are active or regular customers

Of course, there are all sorts of people within each category, young, old, richer, poorer, male, female, and so on.

Because of their different intentions some messages will be general; others will be specific, aimed exclusively at one group or another. In addition, there are the products themselves. To say the promotional and display permutations become numerous is an understatement; in many shops the number of lines stocked is numbered in thousands.

Any change of products to be sold (and therefore displayed), coupled with the customers' tendency to notice only what is new, means displays must regularly be changed or updated. It is there, in part, to remind and to freshen the interest. Again, if you consider your own high street, you may notice, let us say, a window display instantly if it is eye catching (you may even go into the shop and buy something). However, if the window is never changed, it just becomes part of the scenery and, after a while, it makes no impression.

Display, therefore must be carefully carried out to achieve the right effect. There is a mnemonic which demonstrates exactly what needs to be done, AIDA:

87

A – catch the customers' *attention*

I – arouse their *interest*

D – turn their interest into *desire*

A – prompt *action*
(this can be applied to many promotional intentions)

Thus a customer seeing a display of books 'for holiday reading', to take a simple example, has their eye caught by perhaps one aspect of the display – a bucket and spade – and moves from:

— 'what's this'?

— to 'perhaps I do need a book for my holiday'

— to 'that looks just the thing'

— to 'I'll buy it'

This is the essential principle behind good display, and checking a particular display to see if it will carry customers through this kind of sequence is a useful test of its likely effectiveness.

The physical layout of the shop

It is beyond the scope of this book to consider the physical layout of a shop in detail. In any case many aspects are fixed, for a variety of reasons; cost, the lease will not allow change etc. Others are not, and certain basic principles of layout are worth commenting on briefly.

So, in no particular order of importance, consider the following:

- **Traffic flow** – 90 per cent of the population are right-handed and will turn left on entering a shop and tend to go round it clockwise. (This is compounded by habit as so many super-markets and department stores, recognising this, encourage it – it has then become the norm with many of us.)

- **Eyes** – customers select most readily from goods set out at eye level (60–62 inches for a woman, a little higher for men). This puts very high or low shelves at a corresponding disadvantage.

- **Quantity** – customers buy more readily from things displayed in quantity, rather than a single example of a product.

- **Vertical display** – products displayed together are found more manageable if they are above and below each other rather than arranged side by side.

- **Accident** – customers will not pick up, or browse, from any layout that appears accident-prone, i.e. if they think they may not be able to balance an item back in position or that other items may fall, especially if things are fragile.

- **Choice** – customers are attuned to choice. A number of options make this easy to exercise, products sell better from within a range of similar items.

- **Relationships** – customers expect to find related items close at hand (e.g. in a bookshop, dictionaries near books on writing style).

- **Cash points** – these need to be convenient and clearly indicated (and, of course, promptly and helpfully manned; but that is another issue) and can be a focal point for display.

- **Position** – in a large shop, people will walk or search further for things they feel are essential (as has been said it is no accident that bread and sugar are normally at the rear of the super-market). So, if the children's toys are up three flights of stairs, mothers with pushchairs will not make that shop first choice.

- **Colour** – has a fashion, and an image, connotation – bright may be seen as brash – so it must be carefully chosen. This applies to display materials, e.g. a backcloth in the window as well as decoration. Too dull, however, and it is not noticed.

- **Lighting** – must be good, if the product cannot be found or seen clearly no one will buy it, and people's patience is limited.

- **Seating** – some shops want to encourage browsing so, if lack of space does not prohibit, they provide some chairs, and perhaps a stool near the cash point for older customers.

- **Background music** – evokes strong opinions. Some like it, some hate it. However, the reverse, a library-like silence, can be off putting for some. Certainly careful choice and consideration of volume level is necessary.

- **Character** – part of the overall atmosphere will come from the main physical elements of the shop, dark wooden panelling has a quite different feel to more modern alternatives (both may have their place).

- **Floor** – this will be noticed, is it quiet?, can it be kept clean easily? and does it (or should it) direct customer flow as some shops do, using different colours for pathways?

- **Reach** – if things are out of reach, people are reluctant to 'be a nuisance' by asking and may not buy.

- **Signing** – again, as people are reluctant to ask, there must be sufficient signs and all must be clear and direct people easily to everything in the shop. In addition, many signs are virtually in-store advertisements and these can be used to good effect.

- **Standing space** – space to stand and look without completely blocking 'traffic' flow may encourage purchase.

- **Security** – last, but by no means least, this is sadly important in every aspect of retailing from the equipment, e.g. closed circuit TV that may be used, to simple vigilance. Retailing is unfortunately rarely sufficiently profitable to sustain a high level of pilferage without concern.

This list is not, of course, comprehensive, but these and other factors are important and the overall physical construction and layout is the backcloth to any display, in the shop or in the window. Merchandising perhaps demonstrates the need to leave no 'promotional corner' ineffective.

The promotional plan

It is probably clear from all that has now been reviewed about promotion that selecting the 'right' mix and implementing the actual promotional activity is a complex task. So too is deciding how much to spend. Clearly it does not 'just happen'; a systematic approach is necessary, a degree of formality is necessary. Figure 4.4 sets out a classic 12 stage approach, and Figure 4.5 comments on the important issue of setting the budget.

Fig. 4.4 Planning promotional strategy

Any company must:
- Analyse the market and clearly identify the exact need.
- Ensure the need is real and not imaginary, and that support is necessary.
- Establish that the tactics they intend to adopt are likely to be the most cost-effective.
- Define clear and precise objectives.
- Analyse the tactics available, taking into consideration the key factors regarding:
  — the market
  — the target audience
  — the product/service offered
  — the company organisation/resources.
- Select the mix of tactics to be used.
- Check the budget to ensure funds are available.
- Prepare a written operation plan.
- Discuss and agree the operation plan with all concerned and obtain management decision to proceed.
- Communicate the details of the campaign to whoever is implementing it and ensure that they fully understand what they must do, and when.
- Implement the campaign, ensuring continuous feedback of necessary information for monitoring performance.
- Analyse the results, showing exactly what has happened, what factors affected the result (if any) and how much the campaign cost.

Fig. 4.5 Setting the promotional budget

There are several approaches to the complex issue of setting the promotional budget.

1. Percentage of sales

To take a fixed percentage based, usually, on forecast sales relies on the questionable assumption that there is always a direct relationship between promotional expenditure and sales.

It assumes, for example, that if increased sales of 10 per cent are forecast, a 10 per cent increase in promotional effort will also be required. This may or may not be realistic and depends on many external factors. The most traditional and easiest approach, it is also probably the least effective.

2. Competitive parity approach

This involves spending the same amount on promotion as competitive firms or maintaining a proportional expenditure of total 'industry' appropriation or an identical percentage of gross sales revenue compared with competitive firms. The assumption is that in this way market share will be maintained. However, the competition may be aiming at a slightly different sector and including competition in the broadest sense is no help. If you can form a view of competitive/industry activity it may be useful, but the danger of this approach is that competitors' spending represents the 'collective wisdom' of the 'industry', and the blind may end up leading the blind!

It is important to remember that competitive expenditure cannot be more than an indication of the budget that should be established. In terms of strategy it is entirely possible that expenditure should be considerably greater than a competitor's – to drive him out – or perhaps for other reasons, a lot less.

Remember that no two firms pursue identical objectives from an identical base line of resources, market standing etc., and that it is fallacious to assume that all competitors will spend equal or proportional amounts of money with exactly the same level of efficiency.

3. Combining percentage of sales and competitive advertising expenditure

This is a slightly more comprehensive approach to setting the budget, but still does not overcome the problems inherent in each individual method. It does, however, recognise the need for maintaining profitability and takes into account the likely impact of competitive expenditure.

4. What can we afford?

This method appears to be based on the premise that if spending something is right, but the optimum amount cannot objectively be decided upon, the money that is available will do.

Look at:

- what is available after all the other costs have been accounted for, i.e. premises, staff, selling expenses etc.;
- the cash situation in the business as a whole;
- the revenue forecast.

In many companies advertising and promotion are left to share out the tail-end of the budget; more expenditure being considered to be analogous with lower profits. In others, more expenditure on promotion could lead to more sales at marginal cost which in turn would lead to higher overall profits.

Again this is not the best method, demonstrating an ad hoc approach that leaves out assessment of opportunities in both the long and short term.

5. Fixed sum per sales unit

This method is similar to the percentage-of-sales approach, except that a specific amount per unit (e.g. per man-day sold) is used rather than a percentage of pound sales value. In this way, money for promotional purposes is not affected by changes in price. This takes an enlightened view that promotional expenditure is an investment, not merely a cost.

6. What has been learned from previous years?

The best predictor for next year's budget is this year's. Are results as predicted? What has been the relationship of spending to competition? What is happening in the market? What effect is it having and what effect is it likely to have in the future?

- Experiment in a controlled area to see whether the firm is underspending or overspending. As the chairman of a major company once said, 'I know that 50 per cent of our advertising expenditure is wasted, the trouble is I don't know which 50 per cent'.
- Monitor results which is relatively easy, and the results of experiments with different budget levels can then be used in planning the next step (although you must always bear in mind that all other things do not remain equal).

7. Task method approach

Recognising the weaknesses in other approaches, a more comprehensive four-step procedure is possible. Emphasis here is on the tasks involved in the process of constructing a promotional strategy as already described. The four steps of this method are as follows.

- **Analysis**   Make an analysis of the marketing situation to uncover the factual basis for promotional approach. Marketing opportunities and specific marketing targets for strategic development should also be identified.

- **Determine objectives**   From the analysis, set clear short- and long-term promotional objectives for continuity and 'build up' of promotional impact and effect.

92

- **Identify the promotional tasks** Determine the promotional activities required to achieve the marketing and promotional objectives.

- **'Cost out' the promotional tasks** What is the likely cost of each element in the communications mix and the cost-effectiveness of each element?

What media are likely to be chosen and what is the target (i.e., number of advertisements, leaflets etc.)? For example, in advertising, the media schedule can easily be converted into an advertising budget by adding space or time costs to the cost of preparing advertising material. The promotional budget is usually determined by costing out the expenses of preparing and distributing promotional material etc.

The great advantage of this budgetary approach compared with others is that it is comprehensive, systematic and likely to be more realistic. However, other methods can still be used to provide 'ball-park' estimates, although such methods can produce disparate answers. For example:

- we can afford £10,000;
- the task requires £15,000;
- to match competition £17,500;
- last year's spending £8,500.

The decision then becomes a matter of judgement, making allowances for your overall philosophy and objectives.

There is no widely accurate mathematical or automatic method of determining the promotional budget. The task method (number 7) does, however, provide, if not the easiest, then probably the most accurate method of determining the promotional budget.

93

In a large company, or one with a substantial promotional budget, this will be carried out by, or with, an advertising agency with certain of the tasks such as media buying, the creative input, being carried out exclusively by them. It is not necessary, nor is there the space here, to explore this planning process in detail, but it must be done, and done well. Even one simple (simple?) error can cause major problems. For example, you do occasionally see advertising on, say, television for a new product yet are unable to find it in the shops because the manufacturer has got the timing of advertising and stocking out of line. This kind of mistake can not only be costly, but alienate customer loyalty for the future.

Summary

Promotion is, as we have seen, something that encompasses a number of techniques. These need to be deployed against sound objectives, well co-ordinated and – perhaps above all – must be creative.

Though fashion and copying are evident in promotion, and particularly in advertising, originality and creativity are two very important aspects for any successful promotion. A very creative and original scheme, even though inexpensive, can, and often does, score over a high budget, stereotyped uncreative approach. While advertising can never sell a poor product (certainly not more than once), a well thought out and consistent approach can become memorable, advertising slogans even pass into the language; at their best can they create an awareness of a product or service, indeed a desire for it, which may be very difficult for a competitor to overthrow. Even if half the money spent on it were wasted, the other half is very important.

In any case promotion – however good – can be wasted unless backed by effective sales and service, which is the topic of the next chapter.

94

IMPLICATIONS: Review and Action	
Your Job	Related Areas
POINTS TO REVIEW	POINTS TO REVIEW
POINTS TO ACTION	POINTS TO ACTION

5

The personal touch
The role of sales and service

There is an old saying that nothing happens until someone sells something, and in many businesses selling is indeed a vital part of the communications mix without which the rest of the promotional activity can be wasted. Selling, as Figure 4.1 on page 56 showed, is the only persuasive technique which involves direct individual personal contact.

Now selling has an unfortunate image. Think of your own judgement on, say, a double glazing or insurance salesman. The first words that maybe come to mind are 'pushy', 'high-pressure' or 'con-man'. Selling can be associated with pushing inappropriate goods on reluctant customers, selling refrigerators to Eskimos is perhaps the kind of situation which springs to mind in those not directly involved in sales (though eskimos *do* buy refrigerators, they need them to keep food *warm* enough to cook without defrosting! but I digress).

The best selling can be described as 'helping people to buy'. Much of it has advisory overtones and, if it is to be acceptable as well as effective it cannot be pushy, but must, like everything in marketing, be customer orientated. Selling is, in fact, a skilled job and demands a professional approach. Customers may want the product, but with plenty of alternative sources of supply they are demanding and convincing them to do business with a particular supplier may be no easy task.

Perhaps the following apocryphal story (again quoting less

seriously from my book *Everything you need to know about marketing*) makes the difficulty of the task clearer:

Buyers are a tough lot

It is any buyer's job to get the best possible deal for his company. That is what they are paid for, they are not actually on the salesmen's side, and will attempt to get the better of them in every way, especially on discounts.

This is well illustrated by the apocryphal story of the fairground strongman. During his act he took an orange, put it in the crook of his arm and bending his arm squeezed the juice out. He then challenged the audience offering £10 to anyone able to squeeze out another drop.

After many had tried unsuccessfully, one apparently unlikely candidate came forward, he squeezed and squeezed and finally out came a couple more drops. The strongman was amazed, and, seeking to explain how this was possible, asked as he paid out the £10 what the man did for a living. 'I am a buyer with Ford Motor Company' he replied.

Buyers are not really like this; they are worse.

However, and wherever, selling must take place if the marketing process is to be successfully concluded. At one end of the scale it is simple. For example, an off licence may be able to increase sales significantly just by ensuring that every time a member of staff is asked for spirits, they ask, 'How many mixers do you want?' Many people will respond positively to what has been called the 'gin and tonic' effect, the linking of one product with another. Sometimes the question is even simpler: the waiter in a hotel or bar, for example, who asks 'Another drink?'

At the other end of the scale, sales do not come from the single isolated success of one interaction with the customer. A chain of events may be involved, several people, a long period of time and, importantly, a cumulative effect. In other words, each stage, perhaps involving some combination of meetings, proposals, presentations, and more meetings, must go well or you do not move on to the next.

So with the thought in mind that the detail of what is necessary will vary depending on circumstances, let us review both the stages in turn and some of the principles involved in them.

Selling starts, logically enough, with identifying the right people to whom to sell. Sales time is expensive so it is important for sales people to spend time with genuine prospects, the more so when the longer lead time referred to above, and typical in the purchase of, say, computer systems is involved. Some of the right people come forward as a result of promotional activity. They phone up, return a card from a mailshot, or whatever and, in so doing, are saying 'tell me more'. Others have to be found; finding them is the first stage of the selling process.

Locating prospects

This part of the process (which overlaps to some extent with the area of marketing and promotion) is perhaps best described by way of an example. Consider someone in a business all managers probably deal with at some time or another, travel.

99

Walter has a successful retail travel agency business. He identifies that, in addition to selling to customers over the counter, he is well placed to deal with commercial accounts in the area in which his business is located. He needs to initiate some contacts, but with whom? The first stage is to check. He looks at his files, companies he has dealt with previously and individual customers who work for the right kind of company. This produces some names but he needs more and considers a list of sources including:

- *Local Chambers of Commerce and Trade:* not just by consulting their lists but perhaps by belonging to them or addressing their meetings
- *Public libraries:* particularly as a source of some of the items mentioned later in this list
- *His suppliers:* among the companies he buys from, such as office equipment and supplies, there may be potential customers
- *Credit bureaux or other professional service agents*
- *Personal observation:* the factory down the road, the new office block on the corner
- *Local government offices*
- *Referrals:* existing customers, suppliers' customers, contacts or friends
- *His bank*

- *Mailing lists:* often available for rent as well as from directories
- *Exhibitions and trade promotion events*
- *Local hotels:* who already receive business from him and may be helpful in return. What meetings or exhibitions go on there?
- *Company annual reports* (from his public library)
- *Company house/employee magazines* (from his public library)
- *Trade/industry/technical journals* (from his public library)
- *Directories of companies* (from his public library)
- *Telephone directories/yellow pages* (from his public library)

One or a combination of these can supply valuable information about prospects: the names of companies, what business they are in, if it is going well or badly, whether they export, how big they are, who owns them, what subsidiaries or associates they have and, last, but certainly not least, who runs and manages them.

Exactly which individual is then approached is obviously vital, and may not be a simple decision. Indeed, it may be that more than one person is involved. For example, the person who travels, the person who sends him, the person who pays and perhaps also the person who makes the booking. There is many a secretary with considerable discretionary power in making bookings, and not least among their considerations will be how straightforward and easy the travel agency is for them to deal with personally.

As well as considering which individual to approach, the other important assessment at this stage is that of financial potential. How much business might be obtained from them in, say, a year? This analysis will rule out some prospects as not being worth further pursuit. Experience will sharpen the accuracy with which these decisions can be made, but meantime a good first list is developing.

The old military maxim that 'time spent in reconnaissance is seldom wasted' is a good one. In war it can help to prevent casualties. In business it not only produces information on who should be contacted, but provides a platform for a more accurately conceived, and more successful, approach.

So having identified who will be contacted, his next step is *organising the approach*. A number of factors may be important here, both before an approach is made and in follow-up. Two key areas he needs to consider before making an approach are:

- How will the approach be made?

The ultimate objective is almost certainly a face-to-face meeting, which must be held before any substantial business can result. Such a meeting can be set up by:

- 'Cold calling', that is, calling without an appointment
- Sending a letter or card with or without supporting literature
- Telephoning 'cold' or as follow-up to a letter or promotion
- Getting people together, initially as a group, and making a presentation at your premises, a hotel or other venue, or through a third party, (such as at a Chamber of Trade meeting).

The logistics are also important. What is needed is a campaign spread over time so that if and when favourable responses occur they can be followed up promptly; such responses may be more difficult to cope with if they all occur together.

The next consideration is:

- Who will make the approach?

The process will almost certainly involve approaching, meeting and discussing matters with people senior in, and knowledgeable about, their own business. The approach therefore needs to be made by people with the right profile, who will be perceived as being appropriate, and who can really give an impression of competence. They will also need to have the right attitude, wanting to win business in what may be a new and perhaps more difficult area. And they need the knowledge and skills to tackle the task in hand: knowledge of the customers, the agency and its services, of overseas places and processes or the ability to find out quickly. Detail is important. The export manager who is made late for an appointment will be equally upset whether he has missed a flight connection or simply been mis-informed on the time it takes to get from airport to hotel. The travel agent, rightly or wrongly, will probably get the blame. Finally, skills in customer contact, selling and negotiation are needed as well as in all those areas, such as writing sales letters, involved in making the approach. Making the right choice of person is therefore crucial, and in the long term, a small company set on developing its business travel side may need to consider recruitment, training or both.

The initial approach is vital, like any first impression, and it may be very difficult having received an initial negative response to organise a second chance. Having thought the process through in this way, the chances of success are that much greater.

101

However it is set up, once contact occurs, the salesman* has to make and carry through a personal contact and to do this must understand the potential buyers and make his contact both persuasive yet acceptable; in other words not so 'pushy' as to be self-defeating.

Selling is an important element of marketing and it is worth reviewing in some detail just what it entails. Bearing in mind that many jobs involve a degree of persuasion (a link will be made specifically between selling and the job of management towards the end of this chapter), put yourself in the salesman's shoes and see how he must approach the task.

It starts, as was said above, with an understanding of the buyer. No one can sell effectively without understanding how people make decisions to purchase. The thinking which goes on in the buyer's mind goes through seven, distinct, stages:

— *I am important and I want to be respected.*

— *Consider my needs.*

— *How will your ideas help me?*

— *What are the facts?*

— *What are the snags?*

— *What shall I do?*

— *I approve.*

Just think, for a second, what you do faced with a decision to purchase a new refrigerator. You want to deal with someone who is not only polite but concerned for the customer; indeed who is prepared to discover and take on board your needs (what size is necessary to fit the kitchen, what is your view of economy, or price?). Someone whose suggestions helpfully bear in mind the brief, who gives you sufficient information on which to base a decision and is able to handle your queries without becoming defensive or argumentative. And, not least, someone who explains

---

* By salesman I mean the man *or woman* with a full time sales role, what is sometimes called a sales representative. Salesperson may be less sexist, but it implies a greater range of people, a sales assistant in a shop, for instance.

– and makes clear and straightforward – any administrative points (delivery, payment items etc.), allowing you to make a decision confident that you will be pleased with your choice.

Any sales approach that responds unsatisfactorily to any of these stages is unlikely to end in an order. The buying mind has to be satisfied on each point before moving to the next, and to be successful a sales presentation sequence must match the buying sequence, and run parallel to it.

Table 5.1 shows the buying process alongside the sales objectives, what you are trying to achieve at each stage, and the technique employed in any sales communication. The two keys to success are the process of matching the buyer's progression and describing, selectively, the product, and discussing it in a way that relates to precisely what the buyer needs.

In all successful sales, the buyer and the seller would have gone through this sequence stage by stage. If the attempt to sell, which just as often beings with an attempt to buy, is unsuccessful, it will be found that:

103

■ The sequence has not taken place at all

■ Some stage has been missed out

Table 5.1 The buying sequence

How people buy	Sales objective	How to sell: Sales technique
I am important Consider my needs	To explore and identify customer's needs	Opening the sales interview
How will your ideas help me? What are the facts?	To select and present the benefits that satisfy the customer's needs	The sales presentation
What are the snags?	To prevent, by anticipating, snags likely to arise or handle objections raised so that the customer is satisfied with the answers	Handling sales objections
What shall I do? I approve	To obtain a buying decision from the customer or a commitment to the proposition presented	Closing the sale

- The sequence has been followed too quickly or too slowly, which means the seller has allowed it to get out of step with the buying process.

Early on, because the customer needs to go through other stages, the salesman may not always be able to aim for a commitment to buy, but he must have a clear objective on which to 'close' in mind. This may be to get the customer to allow him to send literature, to fix an appointment to meet or to provide sufficient information for a detailed quotation to be prepared. Whatever his objective is, however, it is important to know and be able to recognise the various stages ahead. With any customer contact (by telephone or letter as well as face to face), he can identify:

- What stage has been reached in the buying process
- Whether the selling sequence matches it
- If not, why not?
- What does he need to do if the sequence does not match
- Has a step been missed?
- Is he going too fast?
- Should he go back in the sequence?
- Can his objectives still be achieved, or were they the wrong objectives?
- How can he help the buyer through the rest of the buying process?

Naturally, the whole buying process is not always covered in only one contact between the company and the customer. Every initial contact does not result in a sale, and neither does it result in a lost sale. Some stages of the selling sequence have to be followed up in each sales contact, but the logic applies equally to a series of calls which form the whole sales approach to each customer. For a doubtful customer, or a sale of great complexity and expense, there may be numerous contacts to cover just one of the stages before the buyer is satisfied and both can move on to the next stage. Each call or contact has a selling sequence of its own in reaching the call objectives. Each call is a part of an overall selling sequence aimed at reaching overall sales objectives.

Planning the selling sequence is therefore as much a part of call planning as it is of sales planning, but only rarely does a call take place exactly as planned. Knowing and using the sales sequence and being able to recognise stages of the buying process, are, however, invaluable if salesmen are to realise their potential for direct sales results.

With this basic appreciation of the buyer, and what is directing his reactions, we can look closer at the key areas of the sales approach.

Using product information effectively

Identifying with the buyer, in order to recognise the stages of the buying process and to match them with a parallel selling sequence, must extend to the presentation of the sales proposition. Nowhere is this more important than in the way salesmen look at the product, or service, which they are selling.

Product knowledge is too often taken for granted by companies and sales people. Sadly, experience of hearing hundreds of sales people talking unintelligible gibberish does not support this complacency. Salesmen are too often given inadequate product knowledge and what is given is slanted towards the company, not the customer. Managers are often still heard to say proudly, 'Everyone joining us spends six months in the factory, to learn the business', but many then emerge with no better idea of what the product means *to the customer*. Everyone with any role to play in sales-oriented customer contact must consider the product, and all that goes with it, from the customers' point of view.

Don't sell products, sell benefits.

If salesmen get into the habit of seeing things through the customer's eyes, they will realise that they do not sell special promotions, 'free' trial offers or fancy wrappings do not really sell products either. They sell what customers want to buy.

Customers don't buy promotions or products, they buy benefits.

But what are benefits? Benefits are what products, promotions or services *do* for the customer. It is not as important what the products are, as what they do or mean to the customer.

For example, a person does not buy an electric drill because he wants an electric drill, but because he wants to be able to make holes. He buys holes, not a drill. He buys the drill for what it will do (make holes). And this in turn may only be important to him because of a need for storage and a requirement to put up shelving.

When this is realised, selling becomes more effective and also easier. Salesmen do not have to try to sell the same product to a lot of different people, but meet each person's needs with personal benefits.

Benefits are what things sold can do for each individual customer – the things he wants them to do for him. Different customers buy the same product for different reasons. Therefore, you must identify and use the particular benefits of interest to them.

What a product 'is' is represented by its 'features'.
What a product 'does' is described by its 'benefits'.

If forgotten, then the things that are important to a customer will not always be seen as important from the seller's viewpoint, particularly if he has had little or no sales training. The result can, understandably, end up in a conflict of priorities, as shown in Table 5.2.

Table 5.2 Differing views of seller/customer

Customer	Salesman
Himself: Satisfaction of his needs, eg mortgage to buy a house, new machine to increase production	*Himself:* His company, his products, his ideas
His needs and the benefits that satisfy them	*His product* and making this customer buy it
This salesman: Salesman's company, salesman's products, salesman's ideas	*Benefits* to this customer
Buying from this salesman	*Customer's needs:* Benefits that satisfy this customer's needs

The customer is most unlikely to see things from the seller's point of view. Everyone is to themselves the most important person in the world. Therefore, to be successful, the seller has to be able to see things from the customer's point of view and demonstrate through hs words and actions that he has done so. His chances of success are greater if he can understand the needs of the people he talks to and make them realise that he can help them to fulfil those needs.

To do this necessitates the correct use of benefits. In presenting any proposition to a customer, even simply recommending a product in reply to a query, salesmen should always translate what they are offering into what it will do.

Often, a company, and the people who write the sales literature, grow product-orientated, and gradual product development can reinforce this attitude by adding more and more features. It is only a small step before everyone is busy trying to sell the product on its features alone. It is interesting to note that often, when this happens, advertising and selling become more and more forceful, with the features being given a frantic push, as passing time reveals that there has been no great rush to buy.

Two examples over the years, familiar to everyone, are the audio and camera markets. Stereo equipment, in particular, is almost always promoted on features only. Masses of technical terms, most of them meaningless to the majority of end-users, dominate advertisements and brochures, while the visual communication is based entirely on the appearance of the amplifier, speakers or turntable. Yet what people want from a stereo set is sound and reliability – years of listening pleasure. Cameras are often sold on the same, features orientated, basis.

When competitive products become almost identical in their performance, it can be difficult to sell benefits, since all seem to offer the same benefits. Choice then often depends on the personal appeal of some secondary feature. But even then, there must be emphasis on the benefits of those features, rather than on the features themselves. In 'industrial' selling (to other companies rather than to individual consumers), it is more important than

Table 5.3 Product feature/benefit analysis for an agricultural tractor

Customer needs	Benefits that will satisfy customer needs	Product features from which the benefits are derived
Rational		
(a) Performance – must be able to work fast with a variety of implements	Plenty of power, particularly at low speeds	A 65-BHP diesel engine with high torque at low rpm; wide range of matched implements available
(b) Versatility – must cope with a variety of soil and cultivating conditions	Can travel at a wide variety of speeds	A 10-speed synchromesh gearbox – four-wheel drive available for very difficult conditions
(c) Simplicity – must be easy to operate	Simple and speedy implement changeover; easy to drive	Quick-attach linkage with snap-on hydraulic couplings; ergonomically placed levers and pedals
(d) Low cost – must be economical to run	Low fuel consumption	Efficient engine design with improved braking and fuel injector system; good power/weight ratio
(e) Reliability – must be able to operate continuously and be serviced quickly	Well-proven design with all basic snags removed; local dealer with 24-hour parts service	More than 10,000 units already in operation; wide dealer network with factory-trained mechanics backed by computerised parts operation
Emotional		
(a) Security – (fear of making wrong decision)	Most popular tractor on the market – 10,000 farmers can't be wrong	Largest company in the industry with good reputation for reliability and value for money
(b) Prestige – (desire to gain status in the eyes of others)	Chosen by those engaged in best agricultural practice	Favoured by agricultural colleges and large farmers

Notes

1 The product analysis should be completed from left to right. Only when the needs have been identified can the appropriate benefits and the relevant features be selected.

2 If the salesman works from right to left not only will he lose his buyer's interest as he talks about items which may not be of interest, but also he will have no basis for selecting which benefits to stress.

ever to concentrate on benefits rather than on features, which may be little better than gimmicks. Features are only important if they support benefits that the customer is interested in.

Deciding to concentrate on benefits is only half the battle, however. They have to be the right benefits. In fact, benefits are only important to a customer if they describe the satisfaction of his needs. Working out the needs, and then the benefits, means being 'in the customers' shoes'.

Who is the customer, what are his needs?

To know what benefits to put forward, the salesman must know what the customer's needs are. And to know them, he has to know exactly who the customer is. Very often, the customer is the user – the person who will actually use the product. But frequently, the direct customer is a purchaser or a decision-maker, who is not the user. This is most common in industrial selling, when a buying department is often responsible for ordering as well as handling the purchasing of most of a company's requirements. In consumer products, a manufacturer may sell to a wholesaler, the wholesaler to retailer, and it is only the retailer who actually sells to the users.

109

Naturally, the requirements of the end-user will also be of interest to the various intermediaries, but the best results are going to be obtained if salesmen bear in mind the needs of both the buyer and the user, and the differences between their various needs.

To do this, it is convenient to use a product feature/benefit analysis, which also helps to differentiate features and benefits. Something of this process is shown in Table 5.3. Such an analysis

3 This example is not intended as a complete analysis. That can only be done with a specific buyer in mind as each person has an individual need pattern. Performance will be most important to one farmer, low cost to another.

4 It will be noted that some of the product features are so technical as to be almost meaningless to the layman. This is one of the greatest dangers for the industrial salesman. Unless he translates his trade jargon he will fail to achieve understanding and thus cannot be persuasive.

Reproduced from Patrick Forsyth and Marek Gitlin, *20 Activities for Developing Sales & Effectiveness* (Gower Publishing 1988).

can be produced for each product, or for a product range, and is perhaps particularly useful for new products.

Note that not all the needs will be objective ones. Most buyers, including industrial ones, also have subjective requirements bound up in their decisions. The graph in Figure 5.1 illustrates this concept: the line does not touch either axis as no product is bought on an entirely objective or subjective basis. Sometimes, even with technical products, the final decision can be heavily influenced by subjective factors, perhaps seemingly of minor significance, once all the objective needs have been met.

Matching benefits to individual customer needs makes a sale more likely, for a product's benefits must match a buyer's needs. The features are only what gives a product the right benefits.

By going through this process for particular products, and for segments of the range, and matching the factors identified to customer needs, a complete 'databank' of product information from the customers' viewpoint can be organised.

110

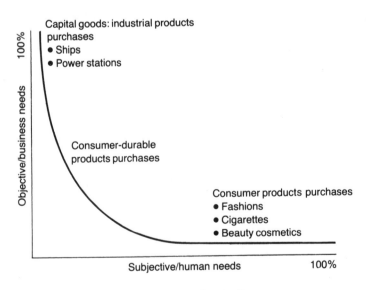

Fig. 5.1 Subjective/objective reasons for buying

Using the benefit approach

With competitive products becoming increasingly similar, more buyers quickly conclude that their main needs can be met by more than one product. Other needs then become more important. If, for instance, a buyer needs a crane, he is likely to find a number of them which will lift the weight required, and which will also cost practically the same.

The deciding factors will then become availability, service and repair facilities, and so on. A seller can look at the 'features' contained by the company as a whole and be ready to convert them to benefits to customers, in the same way as he can practise finding benefits for the full product range. Every aspect of the company and its offering can, potentially, be described in terms of benefits. The headings and examples in Table 5.4 illustrate this:

Table 5.4 Company features and customer benefits

Feature	Customer Benefits	
Products	design price delivery appearance packaging	storage workmanship credit stocks
Services	speed availability credit after-sales service	training advertising merchandising pre-sales advice
Companies	time established reputation location philosophy	labour relations size policies financial standing
Staff	knowledge skill character	availability training specialists

Each item listed in Table 5.4 could be a source of benefit to potential customers, which would help to make them an actual customer. By 'thinking benefits' and by seeing things from the customer's point of view, everyone can make a real contribution to sales and company profitability.

Jargon

A final hazard, which can destroy the customer orientation of sales contacts, is jargon. This 'professional slang' comes in two main forms, both of which can confuse customers:

TECHNICAL OR INDUSTRIAL JARGON

Salesmen should always let the customer be first to use it. Technological complexities have already led to thousands of new words and phrases in business and industry, and introducing still more new terms seldom helps. But worst of all is the possibility that the customer will not know what is being talked about, or will form the wrong impression, yet still hesitate to admit it.

COMPANY JARGON

It is even more important to avoid company jargon, for here the customer will be on very unfamiliar ground. There is a world of difference between 'We'll do a sales/stock return compo and let you know shortly' and 'To answer your query, we'll have to do a comparison of the sales and stock return movements. The quickest way will be to ask for a computer printout which Head Office will forward to us. I will contact you with the answer in a week or ten days' time.'

Company jargon can have a wide effect, not only when used in selling, and even simple phrases can cause trouble. For example, delivery is one area for potential misunderstanding. Promising 'immediate delivery' might mean getting the product to the customer within a week, when normal delivery might take three weeks. But what if the customer is in the pharmaceutical industry, where 'immediate delivery' is jargon for 'within eight hours'? He is almost bound to get the wrong impression.

However saying the right things is not all there is to selling, a critical stage is asking the right questions and listening – *really listening* – to the answer, using these as a guide to how to proceed.

Asking the right questions in the right way

Knowing how and why customers buy is a prerequisite to successful selling, and because all customers are individuals and want to be treated as such, so selling must be based on finding out exactly what each customer wants, and why. In other words, questioning (and listening to and using the answers) is as important to selling as simply presenting the case.

It is important, therefore, to start asking questions early in the approach, and asking the right questions in the right way is crucial. Two characterisitics are important in getting it right. They should be primarily:

- **Open questions:** those that cannot be answered by 'yes' or 'no', but get the customer talking. These work best and produce the most useful information.
- **Probing questions:** those that go beyond enquiring about the background situation, to explore problems and implications, and to identify real needs.

Again we can illustrate this by quoting a possible conversation between the travel agent referred to earlier and one of his prospects.

Agent: 'What areas are currently your priority Mr Export Manager?
Prospect: 'The Middle East is top priority for investigation but, short term, Germany has been more important.'
Agent: 'What makes that so?'
Prospect: 'Well we're exhibiting at a trade fair in Germany. This will tie up a number of staff and eat up a lot of the budget. Our exploratory visit to the Middle East may have to wait.'
Agent: 'Won't that cause problems, seeing as you had intended to go earlier?'
Prospect: 'I suppose it will. With the lead times involved it may rule out the chances of tying up any deals for this financial year.'
Agent: 'Had you thought of moving one of your people straight on from Germany to the Middle East, Mr Export Manager?'
Prospect: 'Er, no.'
Agent: 'I think I could show some real savings over making two separate

113

E

trips. If you did it this way, the lead time wouldn't slip. Would that be of interest?'

Prospect: 'Could be. If I give you some dates can we map something out to show exactly how it could be done?'

Agent: 'Certainly . . .'

This kind of questioning not only produces information but can be used creatively to spot opportunities. It accurately pin-points the prospect's real needs and allows an accurate response to them. Most prospects not only like talking about their own situation but react favourably to this approach. They may well see the genuine identification of their problems and the offer of solutions to them as distinctly different to any competitive approach they have received, which simply catalogues the product or services offered.

In this case, it also allows much better demonstration of two benefits that purchasers look for from travel agents: objectivity and expertise. The more these are apparent, the more the agency is differentiated from the competition.

The professional approach

So far this chapter has concentrated on certain factors inherent in the sales job, particularly those like everything in marketing, which demand a customer orientation and may be relevant to others in the company; these include finding out customer needs and talking benefits. Of course there is more to it than that (in a chapter on selling perhaps I may be forgiven for suggesting my book *The Selling Edge* (Piatkus Books) as a reference for anyone who wants a complete run down on the selling job) so, without going further than the brief for this volume demands let us mention a few more factors.

First, the basics; to be successful, salesmen must be able to:

- *Plan:* they must see the right people, the right number of people, regularly if necessary
- *Prepare:* sales contact needs thinking through, the so-called

'born salesman' is very rare, the best of the rest do their homework

- *Understand the customer:* use empathy, the ability to put themselves in the 'customer's shoes', to base what they do on real needs, to talk benefits
- *Project the appropriate manner:* not every salesman is welcome, not everyone can position themselves as an advisor or whatever makes their approach acceptable
- *Run a good meeting:* stay in control, direct the contact, yet make the customer think he is getting what he wants
- *Listen:* a much undervalued skill in selling
- *Handle objections:* the pros and cons need debating, selling is not about winning arguments or scoring points
- *Be persistent:* asking for a commitment, and, if necessary asking again

115

Secondly, a variety of additional skills may be necessary to operate professionally in a sales role. These include:

- account analysis and planning
- the writing skills necessary for proposal/quotation documents to be as persuasive as face to face contact
- skills of formal presentation
- numeracy and negotiation skills

And all this in a job in which some people say of someone that they are 'only a salesman'.

Before moving on, one last factor which influences sales success deserves a mention, and that is sales management. The sales manager is very much part of the marketing team and has six key tasks and responsibilities, to:

- *Plan:* the scope and extent of the sales operation, its budget and what it will aim to achieve
- *Organise:* defining how many salesmen are required, the kind of staff who are necessary, how and where they are to be deployed

- *Staff:* the recruitment and selection of the best possible team, recognising that the quality of a company's sales team is a factor which can, of itself, differentiate it from its competitors

- *Train:* it has been, wisely, said that 'if you can't train you can't manage'. A social skill such as selling needs both a good foundation of training and constant 'fine-tuning' to maintain high effectiveness in a dynamic market

- *Motivate:* all staff need motivating (something that is no easy task) and in sales it is especially important, as people spend a good deal of time on their own and customers sometimes cause an attrition of attitude in sales people by their demands

- *Control:* constant monitoring is necessary if sales targets are to be met. Action must be taken to anticipate and correct any shortfall, and to build on any successes to maximise profitability in the market place.

116

The chart, Figure 5.5 (developed by my partner David Senton) shows the tasks of sales management diagrammatically. The inner circles (dotted lines) represent short term activity, the outer longer term.

Lastly, in this chapter we will spend a moment on customer service. This, as customers both anticipate and experience it, is fundamental to sales and marketing success.

Customer Care

As has already been mentioned, it is increasingly difficult for customers to differentiate between competing products in the market. In many industries, products are essentially similar in terms of design, performance and specification, at least within a given price bracket. This is as true of industrial products as consumer goods. Often, customers' final choices will, therefore, be influenced by more subjective areas. Customer services can play a major role in this, sometimes becoming the most important factor.

For example, in the author's own business, the source of ring binders used for the many courses and seminars we conduct was,

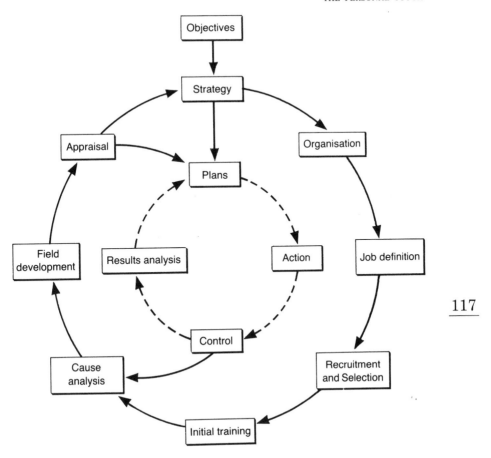

Fig. 5.2 Sales management long/short term tasks and responsibilities

117

for a while, influenced almost exclusively, in a commodity-type product area with many suppliers offering similar products, by the efficiency and customer orientation of one girl in the suppliers' sales office. When she left them, the business was subsequently moved elsewhere. The antithesis of this is the 'abominable noman' who too often seems to inhabit the sales office. He can destroy months of work by management and sales staff, miss opportunities and lose orders, or indeed customers, in a moment, maybe in one brief telephone call. Everyone has their favourite horror story, a fact which may say something about prevailing standards. Any shortfall in prevailing standards presents an opportunity for others in an industry to steal an edge by getting it right. It is not a question of aiming for some idea of perfection (after all both McDonald's restaurants and the Ritz Hotel would claim to offer good service, but in very different ways), but any company must organise positively to achieve the standards they have decided they – or rather their customers – require.

So what creates good customer care? It comes primarily through the careful consideration of both staffing and organisation. It is not easy. The mix of characteristics and considerations that can help make success more likely is not easy to define:

- It is not enough for the manager responsible only to be a good administrator, although without the sorting out of priorities, without smooth handling of enquiries, files, paperwork, correspondence and records, sales support will never be effective.

- It is not enough for him only to be a good sales person, although it is essential to have an understanding or familiarity with sales techniques, be able to recognise sales opportunities, and ensure both he and members of his team meet them.

- It is not enough for him only to be an effective manager of people, although it is vital to be able to lead and motivate a close-knit and enthusiastic team, tackling a diverse range of activity in hectic conditions.

The manager also has to understand and pass on an understanding of the role of sales support, so that all concerned see it as a vital tactical weapon in the overall marketing operation. This means that he must have an appreciation of what marketing is and the various ways in which, directly or indirectly, the sales office, and sales support or customer care staff can contribute to company profitability.

This implies a knowledge of, and involvement in, the marketing process. For example, if sales support personnel are not told (or do not ask about) the relative profitability of different products, they may be busy pushing product 'A' when product 'B', similar in price or even more expensive, makes more money.

A pre-requisite for contributing effectively is for any manager to be able to identify priorities. With such a variety of activities, with incoming calls and enquiries being so unpredictable, the manager either adheres to rigid sets of rules that allow things to be coped with and runs an adequate office, or he has the skill and initiative to recognise different priorities and to get the best out of them, so building up a really effective operation.

Identifying priorities is of little use, however, unless the manager is able to organise to deal with them. This calls for abilities in managing and controlling time, systems and people.

To be effective he must be a consistent sales-oriented manager of people, able to accept ideas from others, able to cope with the problems of the urgent and balance this with the opportunities of the important.

The sales support team must be organised to produce an ongoing positive cycle of repeat business from its contacts. Even negative contacts such as complaints can be dealt with as part of a positive cycle involving a range of possible contacts with the customer, either directly or through other sections of the company. Although possibly low among company priorities, sales support in fact occupies a central position, which is vital in terms of contacts and influence.

For this to occur may require close and constructive co-operation with other sections of the company for example, production, or the sales force. Poor liaison can cause problems. In one company, for instance, sales office staff spent time handling complaints about delivery on 75 per cent of orders that went through, not because delivery was bad, but because the sales force was quoting six weeks delivery when everyone in the company knew it was normally eight weeks. Such unnecessarily wasted time could be used more constructively to increase sales.

There are, of course, exceptions. Prevailing standards of sales office service and selling are not high. It should not be difficult, therefore, to make customer contact not only stand out in a way that really impresses customers but which genuinely increases sales results. For many firms, this is a real opportunity area that is too often neglected.

There are no excuses for not selling. Time pressure, work pressure, staffing, equipment and resources may all make it more difficult, but what in fact ensures real selling does take place is, first, attitude and, second, skills and knowledge of how to do it effectively. Only management can get this over and maintain standards. It is, in fact, much easier to run a 'tight ship' to set standards and stick to them than to let things go by default. People are motivated by belonging to the 'best team' and come to care about standards and performance very much.

Selling must not be confused with simple customer service, however efficient and courteous. This is not to deny the vital importance of service and courteousness. This forms one of the bases for success, but so does product knowledge – not just knowing about the product, but being able to talk about it in such a way that makes sense to the customer. This does not just happen. Management must ensure that it does, and similarly with sales technique. The sales office team (all of them who have customer contact) must have a basic knowledge of the sales process augmented by knowledge of and ability to apply particular skills, on the telephone or in letter writing for instance, and backed as necessary by sheer persistence and inventiveness. Again, this does not just happen. Management is responsible for recruiting the right people, their initial training and on-going development, and for

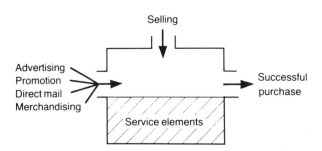

Fig. 5.3 Sales are the net result of promotion, selling and good service

motivating them on a continuous basis. As with so many topics reviewed here, customer service and the internal sales effort have more to them than meets the eye. Yet think about organisations you do business with, as a company or as an individual. There is always one about which you say 'never again!' and others where good service draws you back time after time, probably without your thinking that you have been sold to in a 'pushy' manner.

Promotion, selling and customer care act together to produce the right level of business; this is illustrated in Figure 5.3, as if the various influences were water flowing into a tank, the outflow (sale) is the next result of them all.

Postscript: holding and developing customers

There is an old saying that 'selling starts when the customer says yes' meaning that any company wanting long-term, repeat business, must work at it. Again, the principles can be illustrated by reference to the travel agent Walter.

121

Holding and developing customers

Walter knows that in winning more business travel the overall objective is not one order, but on-going profitable business from this area. Whether customers are retained, buy again and buy more is dependent primarily on two factors:

- *Service:* It almost goes without saying, but promises of service must be fulfilled to the letter; if they are not, the customer will notice. A number of different people may be involved in servicing the account. They all have to appreciate the importance and get their bit right.
  If the customer was promised information by 3.30pm, a visa by the end of the week, two suggested itineraries in writing and a reservation in a certain hotel at a particular price, then he should get just that. Even minor variations, such as information by 4pm and a slight price difference on room rate, do matter. Promise what can be done. And do it 100 per cent.
- *Follow-up:* Even if the service received is first class, the customer must continue to be sold to after the order as follows:
  - Check with him after his trip.
  - Check who else is involved in the next purchase. His secretary? Other managers?

- Ask more questions. When is his next trip? When should he be contacted again?
- Make suggestions. Can he book earlier? Would he like to take his wife on his next trip?
- Anticipate. Does he know fares are going up? Can he make the trip earlier and save money?
- Explore what else he might buy.
- Investigate who else in the company travels. Other staff, departments, subsidiaries?
- See whether you can distribute holiday information among his staff.
- Write to him, do not let him forget you. Make sure he thinks of you first.

A positive follow-up programme of this sort can maximise the chances of repeat business and ensure that opportunities to sell additional products or services are not missed.

IMPLICATIONS AROUND THE COMPANY (5)

Influence of backup on sales

Sales people may succeed or fail largely through their own personal approaches, but they are necessarily dependant on the quality of the product or service which they sell, and the image of the company for which they sell it. So, if your job is involved with anything to do with either, then you help influence sales success.

This is more than saying that those on the production line are involved, there are many more specific circumstances. Consider a few examples:

- Someone in technical support, handling a customer query, will not only sort out the problem, but influence the likelihood of a customer reordering;
- Someone responsible for originating a computer system which, ultimately, interfaces with customers will affect company image and thus the sales persons relationship with their customers;
- Someone in accounts, sorting out some complexity of VAT on a customer account, affects their image of the company for good or ill.

In some of these areas the normal expectation, and experience, of the customer is that any good impression of the company will be diluted. Who hearing the words 'it's in the computer' does not expect some inconvenience their end? What are the equivalents of all this in your own organisation?

More generally, because selling is essentially only persuasive communication, it is, to a degree, true to say that everyone sells something. Much communication around a company is less than straightforward (remember the different view inherent in the business, Table 1.2, p. 7) and, while not directed at customers, must still be persuasive; making it so utilises exactly the techniques reviewed in this chapter.

A 'mini-case' example will help make the point. Consider the following situation.

Mr B runs the sales office for a medium-sized company. His team take customer enquries, offer technical advice, handle queries of all kinds and take orders. Recent reorganisation has resulted in the merging of two departments. His people now occupy a large office together with the order processing staff, who see to the invoicing and documentation. For the most part, all is going smoothly. However, the routing of telephone calls has become chaotic. The switchboard, despite having a note explaining who handles customers in which area of the country, is putting two out of three calls through to the wrong person, and the resulting confusion is upsetting staff and customers alike as calls have to be transferred.

123

Mr B carefully drafts and sends a memo to the Personnel Manager, to whom the switchboard operators report, complaining that the inefficiency of their service is upsetting customers and putting the company at risk of losing orders. He is surprised to find that far from the situation improving, all he gets is a defensive reply listing the total volume of calls with which the hard-pressed switchboard has to cope, quoting other issues as of far more importance at present to the Personnel department and suggesting he takes steps to ensure customers ask for the right person.

Mr B intended to take prompt action that would improve customer service, he felt he had stated his case clearly and logically, yet all he succeeded in doing was rubbing a colleague up the wrong way. The problem remained.

Think how else it might be handled before reading on.

Here the core of the communication is in writing. The memo Mr B sent, though well-intentioned, had the wrong effect, and would also have made any follow-up conversation (necessary because the problem had still to be resolved) more difficult.

From the way the example is first stated, we can imagine the sort of memo that was sent, probably something along the following lines:

Memorandum

To: Ms X, Personnel Manager   3 March
From: Mr B, Sales Office Manager

Subject: Customer Service

A recent analysis shows that, since the merging of the sales office and order processing departments, two out of three incoming calls are misrouted by the switchboard and have to be transferred.

This wastes time and, more important, is seen by customers as inefficient. As the whole intention of this department is to ensure prompt, efficient service to our customers, this is not only a frustration internally, it risks reducing customers' image of the organisation and, at worst, losing orders.

I would be grateful if you could have a word with the supervisor and operators on the switchboard to ensure that the situation is rectified before serious damage results.

124

The problem is certainly identified, the implications of it continuing are spelt out, a solution – briefing of the relevant staff by the Personnel Manager – is suggested. The intention, as has been said, is good. However, despite a degree of politeness – 'I would be grateful . . .' – the overall tone of the message is easy to read as a criticism. Further the solution is vague, tell them what exactly? It seems to be leaving a great deal to Personnel. Maybe he felt 'it is not my fault, *they* should sort it out'. To an extent this may be true, but you may find you often have to choose between a line which draws attention to such a fact or which sets out to get something done. They are often two different things.

In this case the key objective is to change the action, and to do so quickly before customer relations are damaged. This is more important than having a dig at Personnel, and worth taking a moment over. It is, whilst a matter of overall company concern, something of more immediate concern to the sales office.

So what should Mr B have done? To ensure attention, collaboration and action, his memo needed to:

- Make the problem clear
- Avoid undue criticism, or turning the matter into an emotive issue
- Spell out a solution
- Make that solution easy and acceptable to those in Personnel (including the switchboard operators themselves)

Perhaps with that in mind, his memo should have been more like the following:

Memorandum

To: Ms X, Personnel Manager   3 March
From: Mr B, Sales Office Manager

Subject: Customer Service

The recent merger of the sales office and order processing departments seems to have made some problems for the switchboard.

You will find that I have set out in this note something about what is happening and why, and specific suggestions to put it right. You will see the suggested action is mainly with myself, but I would like to be sure that you approve before proceeding.

The problem
Two out of every three calls coming in are misrouted and have to be transferred. This wastes time both in my department and on the switchboard and is likely to be seen as inefficient by customers. To preserve customer relations, and perhaps ultimately orders, it needs to be sorted out promptly.

The reason
Apart from the sheer volume of calls, always a problem at this time of the year, the problem is one of information. The switchboard operators have insufficient information to help guide them, and what they do has been outdated by the departmental merger. Given clear guidance neither they, nor customers, will have any problems.

Action
What I would suggest, therefore, are the following actions:

1 I have prepared a note (and map) showing which member of staff, deals with customers from which geographic area, and would like to make this available for reference on the switchboard.

2 This might be best introduced at a short briefing and if we could assemble the operators for ten minutes before the board opens one morning, I could do that with them and answer any questions.

3 Longer term, it would be useful if the operators visited our department and saw something of what goes on, we could arrange a rota and do this over a few lunch hours so that it can be fitted in conveniently.

If this seems a practical approach do let me know and I will put matters in hand.

125

This is not set out as the 'right' or guaranteed approach, but it is certainly better. And it is more likely to work because it follows the rules, right back to the seven steps set out earlier in this chapter. Especially:

- It lays no blame
- It recognises that Personnel, and the switchboard are important
- It considers their needs – for clear guidance, being able to handle the volume more easily, someone else taking the action
- It anticipates objections, who will do all this, for instance
- It is specific in terms of action, who will do what.

There seems every chance it will have the desired effect. Many situations exhibit similar characteristics. All it needs is a clear, systematic approach that recognises the other person's point of view, and *sells* the desired action. Try it, you might be surprised at how well it works.

126 Summary

Everything commented on in this chapter comes down to one thing; people. Without an effective sales team, and sales management and back up; without an attitude that ranks customer care and good service as a priority around the company; every other activity of marketing is at risk. If promotion is well thought out, creative and powerful; if selling is effective and customer orientated and it is backed by caring service even an average product may sell well; and a good one can then be a winner that leaves competitors behind.

IMPLICATIONS: Review and Action	
Your Job	Related Areas
POINTS TO REVIEW	POINTS TO REVIEW
POINTS TO ACTION	POINTS TO ACTION

6

Moving it down the chain

Distributive processes and options

However good the product or service, however well promoted and however much customers – potential customers – want it, it has to be got to them; distributed. And this is a complex business. Consider the variety of ways in which goods are made available. Consumer products are sold in shops, retailers, but these may vary enormously in nature, from supermarkets and department stores, to specialist retailers, general stores and market traders. These may, in turn, be located in a town or city centre, in an out of town shopping area, in a multistorey shopping centre, or on a neighbourhood corner site.

But the complexity does not stop there, retailers may be supplied by a network of wholesalers or distributors, or they may simply be not involved; some consumer products are sold by mail order, or door to door, or through home parties (like Tupperware). A similar situation applies to services, even traditional banking services being made available in stores, from machines in the street and through post and telephone – even on a drive-in basis. Business to business, industrial products are similarly complex in the range of distributive options they use.

An example quickly shows the complexities and links and 'chains' involved. Figure 6.1 shows on a flowchart basis the way in which books (like this one, perhaps) are marketed. Even this is simplified. There are several kinds of wholesaler, the educational category could well be expanded to include professional bodies (such as the Institute of Management with whom the publishers

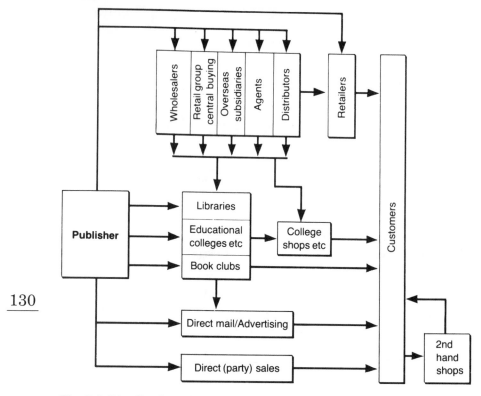

Fig. 6.1 Distributive 'chains' in publishing

publishers of this book work on a series basis) and retailers can include everything from a major book shop, to quite different kinds of shops which sell some books, from supermarkets to guide books sold in tourist offices.

Given all this complexity and the many options, deciding organising and managing the chosen option (or options) is an important task. Clearly, as Figure 6.1 showed, distribution can involve a number of levels – or steps, as they are sometimes referred to – and therefore involve large numbers of external organisations and people. Why, one may ask, given that some organisations do deal direct with customers, should intermediaries be involved at all?

There are, in fact, a number of good reasons for delegating what is an essential element of the marketing mix, for example:

- Distributive intermediaries provide a ready-made network of contacts that would take years to establish at what might be a prohibitive cost.

- Distributors provide an environment that the customer needs in order to make a choice. If different competing brands need to be compared, this can be done by the customer in the supermarket. If a local firm or a well-known distributor stocks a product, it may enhance the credibility of product in the eyes of a consumer by association.

- Distributors can spread the costs of stocking and selling one product over all the brands they carry, thereby distributing it at a lower cost than you can.

- The cost of bad debts is sometimes lower than it would be otherwise, as the distributor effectively shares the risk.

- Since the distributor is rewarded by a discount off the selling price, no capital is tied up in holding local stocks.

- Distributors have good specialist knowledge of retailing or distribution, which the principal may not possess.

131

So far so good, but (there is always a but):

- They are not as committed to a product as the producer is. If the customer prefers another, they will substitute it.

- They may use the manufacturer's product as a loss leader.

- They may drop the product from their list if they believe they can make a better profit with another line.

- They expect the manufacturer to stimulate demand for the product; for example, by advertising or providing display material.

The question of whether to deal direct with the consumer is, therefore, dependent first upon the availability of suitable channels and their willingness to add additional products to the range they sell. Secondly, on balancing the economies of the distributors' lower selling and servicing costs with the disadvantages of not being present at the point where customers are making their decisions, and thus having less control over the selling process.

What channel of distribution to choose

Although this is, as we have seen already, a decision involving some complex, interlocking issues, six main factors will influence the route taken:

Customer characteristics: distributors are generally required when customers are widely dispersed, there is a large number of them and they buy frequently in small amounts.

Product characteristics: direct distribution is required when bulky products, such as soft drinks, are involved. Bulky products need channel arrangements that minimise the shipping distance and the number of handlings.

Where high unit value can cover higher unit selling costs, manufacturers can keep control over distribution by dealing direct. Finally, products requiring installation or maintenance are generally sold through a limited network, such as sole agents.

Distributor characteristics: distributors are more useful when their skills of low cost contact, service and storage are more important than their lack of commitment to one product or brand. For example, some manufacturers of hardware find this is true where their brands have little effect on their customer loyalty.

Competitive characteristics: the channels chosen may often be influenced by the channels competitors use. For example, some manufacturers seek to place their product close to that of their competitors: Burger King try to obtain sites next to McDonald's. On the other hand, some manufacturers, such as Avon Cosmetics, choose not to compete for scarce positions in retail stores and have established profitable door-to-door direct selling operations instead.

Company characteristics: the size of a company often correlates with its market share. The bigger its market share, the easier it is to find distributors willing to handle the product. Paradoxically, the more powerful a manufacturer is, the less he needs to rely on distributors. For example, if a manufacturer has ample financial resources at his disposal, he may decide to cover all marketing functions himself and to delegate only a small proportion of the functions to the distributors. A manufacturer of small domestic appliances, for example, may decide to make his own arrangements for after-sales service, rather than leave it to his dealers.

Additionally, a policy of fast delivery is not compatible with a large number of stages in the channel and there is a tendency to deal direct, if this is important.

Environmental characteristics: changes in the economic and legal environment can also bring about changes in distributive structures. For example, when the market is depressed, manufacturers want to move their goods to market in the most economic way. They thus cut out intermediaries or unessential services to compete on price and deal direct. Again, legal restrictions have been introduced in the UK in recent years to prevent channel characteristics which 'may tend to substantially lessen competition'.

133

Finally, there may be legal restrictions on who may handle the product. For example, ethical drugs, those available on prescription, may only be sold through chemists and chemists' wholesalers.

Usually it is possible to identify several different types of channel or distributors. A firm deciding to market car radios, for example, has the following alternatives:

- *Original equipment market:* it could seek a contract with one or more car manufacturers to buy its radios for factory installation on their cars.
- *Car dealer market:* it could sell the radios to various car dealers for replacement sales when they service cars.
- *Retail automotive parts dealer market:* it could sell its radios to the public through retail automotive parts dealers. It could reach these dealers through its own sales force or via wholesalers.
- *Specialist car radio outlets:* selling nothing else.

- *Retailers specialising in a range of electronic equipment into which car radios fit* (e.g. Dixons).

- *Mail order market:* It could arrange to have its radio advertised in mail order catalogues and the DIY press.

And many more.

Each alternative would be explored to see which channel or combination of channels best met the firm's objectives and constraints. However, the best choice of channel must take into account whether the manufacturer can control the distribution channel he has created.

Distribution management

Not only are chosen distributors likely to work better on behalf of a manufacturer if communications, support (e.g. information, training, technical service) and motivation are good, but they will have their own ideas and a good working relationship must be adopted if both are to profit from the partnership. All this takes time.

We will review, briefly, a number of issues which must be addressed in this area. Usually, a manufacturer expects the 'distributors' to buy the goods for resale and take on the risks and costs of:

- Storage and delivery
- Shrinkage (i.e. loss from damage or theft)
- Bad debts.

As the distributor is using his own capital, he is highly motivated to move the stock, and so plays an active part in selling the goods. Although the 'stockist' also buys the goods on his own account in response to requests from his customers, he expects the manufacturer to ensure high demand and, when this does not materialise, expects to be able to return the goods.

An 'agent', however, only takes the goods on consignment; that is although the goods may be on his premises, they remain the property of the manufacturer and the attendant risks remain with the manufacturer. Since his capital is not at risk, the agent is happy to sell to customers who may not pay, and instead of acting for the manufacturer, he refers all customer complaints back.

So, unless a clear, mutual understanding is reached as regards each partner's duties when setting up the distributive agreement, there will inevitably be problems and conflict.

Thus, the definition of the type of distributive role involved is important; although this may take many forms such arrangements normally fall into three categories:

Sole agency: this agreement is common when a distributor is required to make a substantial commitment or investment to provide services solely for one product or brand. To protect both parties, the distributor agrees not to stock competitive items and the manufacturer agrees not to appoint another distributor within the local area.

135

Exclusive distribution: this is common when a manufacturer wishes to protect the image of his product by channelling it through a limited number of outlets, even though these distributors are stocking competitive brands. For example, a manufacturer of expensive watches may undertake in his agreement with his jewellers who will retail his watches not to sell through department stores and only to appoint a limited number of jewellers as distributors.

Extensive distribution: certain FMCG products benefit from being placed alongside their competitors wherever they are displayed. Manufacturers of such products want their goods available in every suitable store in the country, but the number of such stores is finite.

Other products such as cigarettes and chewing gum need to be available to their consumers in every place by every possible means, such as corner shops, supermarkets, bars, hotels, trains, automatic dispensers, etc. Both manufacturer and distributor understand the need for such a policy and the benefit to both parties.

Before leaving the subject of distribution, three other elements of it are worth a mention.

The first is the way distribution systems can concentrate *power*. In some product areas a large proportion of total business goes through a small number of large distributors, as in the way in which for any product sold through supermarkets, in the UK the top four or five chains will probably sell two thirds of the manufacturer's output. To exploit the market to any real extent, a manufacturer *has* to trade with them. Similar situations exist also in industrial markets; sometimes the distributor will exploit the power this gives to:

- Squeeze preferential discounts from manufacturers. These are sometimes then used to cut the price of the product.

- Force manufacturers to produce similar products to his own for the distributor. The distributor then sells these 'own brands' at a lower price. (Such own brands are a major feature of many markets).

- Limit the manufacturers' role to that of producing goods to the distributor's specification at the lowest possible mark-up.

Note: This is an example of what is called Pareto's Law, so called after an Italian mathematician of that name, or the '80/20 rule'. This refers to the common occurrence of, in this case, 80 per cent of sales and/or profit coming from 20 per cent of customers. The numbers will not be exact, but this kind of ratio occurs in a number of areas of marketing (others include product range and mix) and prompts organisational action. Many companies manage major customers on a different basis from more normal sized ones and have staff with titles such as 'Major Account Executive' so to do; this is sensible as major customers are not just different in scale, but in nature.

The second is *overseas markets*. Generally speaking the more widely a product can be distributed geographically the more will be sold. There used to be a much quoted maxim 'export or die', certainly a nation's balance of payments is made healthier if exports are high. In the UK despite all the exhortation to export, some 90 per cent of total exports (by value) is sold by a few hundred organisations within the country. Not only products are involved, of course, many services produce foreign currency too. These include banking, insurance, travel services (e.g. airlines) and even consultancy (the author, amongst others, is, on occasion, what is referred to as an 'invisible export' conducting training courses for organisations in a number of different countries).

All the principles of marketing apply overseas. Without going into too much detail electing to define two areas of activity as follows indicates the scope involved.

- *Export marketing* is essentially selling goods to overseas customers, often through distributors or agents, but doing so from base.
- *International marketing* implies a greater involvement in the overseas territories, everything from setting up subsidiaries, licensing (giving others permission to manufacture, usually on a royalty basis) to joint ventures.

137

Some companies sell what they produce worldwide, others tailor the product to individual markets – even something as simple as a chocolate bar may have many different recipes and flavours for each of many different markets.

The marketing principle of 'knowing your customer' is clearly paramount in overseas markets where people, culture, customs and more may be very different. Such differences will not only potentially affect the product specification, some technical, such as different safety legislation; or fashion (a colour may be popular in one country and regarded as unlucky in another), but the manner of doing business. The prevailing practice regarding negotiation, business ethics or time scale may all be different. Even a brand name may need careful checking; what sounds catchy in English may be lewd in Urdu. Another key factor of marketing overseas is the increased commitment; people, resources, money are all spread more widely.

The third additional element to mention is *physical distribution*. Marketing and sales create demand, the process of making sure goods get to the customer on time and in perfect condition, is called 'physical distribution'.

A comprehensive description would be – physical distribution management is the term describing the integration of two or more activities for the purpose of planning, implementing and controlling the efficient flow of raw materials, in-process inventory and finished goods from point of origin to point of sale and consumption. These activities may include, but are not limited to, customer service, demand forecasting, distribution communications, inventory control, material handling, order processing, part and service support, plant and warehouse site selection, procurement, packaging, return goods handling, salvage and scrap disposal, traffic and transportation, warehousing and storage. From this it will be obvious how closely sales and physical distribution should work together to ensure maximum efficiency in achieving results and maintaining reliability in meeting orders. Each link in the chain between initial enquiry, order placing, manufacturing or goods from stock process, packaging, transport and delivery to the customer must be under constant scrutiny or costs and prices will quickly get out of control.

138

Some of these, customer service for instance, overlap specifically with marketing and may come under the control of an aspect of it – the sales department say. Some have a dual role. Packaging has to protect the goods, meet additional specifications such as a facility to be stacked safely and conveniently on a display and performs a promotional function – the pack is a mobile advertisement (and a purveyor of information, some technical). In most organisations the management of the physical distribution process will not be directly run by marketing; the overlap and the importance of marketing success however, are clear. Something arriving late and broken will not begin to persuade the customer to buy again. Something arriving promptly, safely and in a way which adds to the attractiveness of the whole deal, well might.

IMPLICATIONS AROUND THE COMPANY (6)

Implementation overlap

In any successful company change is afoot continuously. In one company, selling grocery products, two changes were in progress in parallel.

First, the marketing department was implementing a new price structure. The main change was to the discount break points, that is, in a business where products were ordered by the case, the point at which unit price changed. So, let us say up to 100 cases were one price each, but for a quantity of 101–200 the unit price was a little lower, and so on. This worked well, and the new scale was designed, not least, to help the sales team achieve higher order sizes with attendant economies of scale, and a lower likelihood of retailers becoming out of stock of any particular item in the range.

Secondly, the distribution department, who ran their own fleet of trucks, were re-equipping with new vehicles. While this was a major investment, there would be long term savings in cost.

Both eminently reasonable.

Except that several of the main likely order sizes no longer fitted the trucks. Five hundred cases were now a truck and a small bit. Distribution began dispatching such orders, less a small percentage (it being uneconomical to send a larger truck or a second delivery) and immediately complaints started to come in about inaccurate delivery. A costly sorting out was, in fact, avoided as the problem was spotted early on. But time and money was wasted because neither side had considered implications in parts of the operation outside their immediate sphere of influence; the result was something customers read as inefficiency.

A classic case of how understanding between departments can assist marketing activity. It might be wrong to lay blame on one side or the other in such a case, but the opportunity to make the changes more smoothly was there to be grasped by someone.

139

Summary

Distribution is a vital process that links the company to customers, marketing activity can be made or broken by its performance.

The right method must be chosen, and then any distributors worked with effectively. Few distributors will even consider taking on a new product unless they can be convinced that the market research has been done and the demand exists. They need to know which market segment the product is aimed at and whether it fits their customer franchise.

Working through any channel of distribution demands clear policy; that all parties have clear, understood and agreed expectations of each other; ditto terms of trade (discounts and all financial arrangements); that sufficient time and resources are put into the on going process of managing, communicating with and motivating those organisations and people upon whom sales are ultimately dependent.

IMPLICATIONS: Review and Action	
Your Job	Related Areas
POINTS TO REVIEW	POINTS TO REVIEW
POINTS TO ACTION	POINTS TO ACTION

7

Pulling together
Co-ordination, control and culture

This is intentionally a short chapter, not because the factors to which it refers are unimportant (they are crucial), but because the detail of what is involved is of less relevance to others. A number of matters are, however, worth brief comment.

Organising the marketing function

In order to achieve its objectives, some form of planning system is needed. This, in turn, demands an organisation structure both to create marketing plans and to implement them.

Being a *marketing* organisation (i.e. consumer needs orientated), the structure should be built from the bottom up. This process starts by identifying what services consumers desire from the company in order to be persuaded to buy. This will help specify the nature and scale of, for example, the sales effort required.

Likewise, the management structure of this field operation can be identified by asking, What support do the subordinates need in terms of nature and scale in order that their activities are effective and controlled?

Whatever the form of marketing organisation adopted, care must be given to its integration with other functions of the company.

Control in marketing is conceptually similar to other forms of management control. It depends upon the comparison of Actual performance against pre-set Standards and the taking of corrective action based upon the resulting Variances i.e.

$$A - S = \pm V$$

The objectives and plans will form the basis of the standards. Thus, the sales plan will contain sales forecasts which can be translated into targets for each salesman.

Many of the promotion areas have been traditionally viewed as immeasurable. Undoubtedly it is difficult to assess and control activities which for the large part depend upon human reaction and which cannot be easily separated from other influences. The difficulty has been exacerbated, however, by attempting to evaluate each part in terms of the whole. Thus, 'How much will advertising affect sales?' is usually an unanswerable question as sales do not depend upon advertising alone.

144   If, however, it is clearly specified what the advertising is supposed to do i.e. impress a certain message on a certain number of people of a certain type, then it is feasible to define standards of performance and evaluate achievement.

Certainly, control of a different kind can and should be exercised in marketing. All marketing activities are quantifiable in money terms and thus budgetary control can be exercised.

For marketing activities to be effective it is not enough that each department should be well run. The whole marketing function needs to be integrated and well co-ordinated with the rest of the company.

Implementing and controlling the plan

A marketing plan, deriving from a SWOT analysis and the other processes referred to in Chapter 2, should spell out three key elements of the activity that it plans. These are: objectives, strategies and tactics; these are illustrated in Table 7.1.

Table 7.1 Planning elements

Concepts	Illustrations	Contents
Objectives	The corporate *destination*	What needs to be achieved. This must be expressed by objectives which are: S . . . Specific M . . . Measurable A . . . Achievable R . . . Realistic T . . . Timed
Strategies	The *road* the company will travel to reach its destination	A description of how the company will achieve its objectives: S . . . Segments A . . . Audience P . . . Product features/ benefits
Tactics	The *vehicle* used to carry the company along its strategic road	A description of: P . . . People responsible A . . . Actions to be completed M . . . Methods to be employed

145

Successful implementation depends upon the effective management of five resources:

- *What*: the goals, objectives, aims
- *Who*: the people responsible/accountable for plan realisation
- *Where*: the specific, identified, quantified market places
- *When*: the period covered by the plan
- *Why*: the reasons, desired outcomes

It will be perhaps a marketing manager's responsibility to ensure that all material marketing resources are in place. These could well comprise:

F

Table 7.2 Marketing plan control

Type of control	Objective of control	Standards	How to measure performance	What to look for examples:
1. Annual product plan control	To examine if plan objectives are being achieved	Sales quotas and market share financial targets	Comparison of actual results against standards set in each area of performance	Notable shortfall between standard and actual; failure of individual sales territories to achieve sales targets by buyer category
2. Profitability control	To examine if financial objectives are being met	Profitability by product or product group	Comparison of actual results against standards	Major shift in production mix; spending levels above plan levels; declining sales
3. Efficiency/productivity control	To evaluate and improve results of marketing expenditures	Promotional deadlines. Distribution targets. Sales force activities.	Comparison of actual results against advertising plan; sales force: who called on/how many/call frequency/what done in each call	Failure to meet deadlines or set standards in each area of promotion

- Product
- Packaging
- Internal promotion aids (sales aids)
- External promotion campaigns (e.g. advertising)
- Budgetary management systems
- Sales data systems
- Performance standards

Once the plan is launched, the emphasis of attention changes to *control*. The plan should contain specific financial, marketing, sales, distribution and promotion objectives. These provide a basis for performance standards in a number of key areas, including product sales (in value terms), product sales (in volume terms) and product sales (in market share terms).

Performance standards can be expressed as follows:

147

- **Annual targets:** these express performance expectations in sales, profit and market share terms. Annual targets are known as *absolute targets*. Variances to these targets will identify what has gone right or wrong, but not why.
- **Moving standards:** these express the annual targets in moving divisions of the plan period i.e. monthly or quarterly actuals, cumulatives and trends. Again, although moving standards can forecast deviations from plan, they will not identify why performance is greater or less than the required targets.
- **Diagnostic standards:** these *can* identify what and why is causing the variations, and may indicate an appropriate action.

Table 7.2 amplifies these points

VARIANCE ANALYSIS

Variances are calculated by comparing actual results against the pre-set standards.

First, use cumulative totals so that individual monthly variations will tend to cancel each other out.

Secondly, moving annual totals (MATs) can be used by taking 12 months' performance up to and including the month in question. As each month is added and the same month of the previous year is deducted, the trend in *moving annual total* will indicate present performance compared with the same period in the previous year.

This enables comparisons to be made on a single diagram of monthly performance against target, cumulative performance against target and, via the moving annual total, the present year versus the previous year.

The benefit of a good control system and feedback mechanism is that it enables a manager to quickly identify *sales performance variances and the true reasons for them*, and to *react to changed circumstances*. By controlling the Plan he will be in a position to report monthly, and answer the following questions which may be raised by top management:

148

- Are the plan objectives being met?
- What are the variances between budget and actual?
- What are the causes of these variances?
- What actions are being taken to correct them?
- Is a re-forecast/re-budget necessary?

Marketing will not guarantee success but carefully applied it will certainly increase the likelihood.

Note: in a commercial environment, an organisation's success is measured by its profitability. For those interested in how this is defined, the text below sets out further detail (this is adapted from the chapter 'Finance and the Sales Manager' in a book I edited for Gower Publishing: *The Sales Management Handbook*).

The profit mechanism

The best overall measurement of corporate performance is usually taken to be return on capital employed (R/CE). This ratio is calculated by expressing net profit (usually before tax) (R) as a percentage of capital employed (CE). Capital employed is calculated by taking the total assets less the current liabilities, which is of course equivalent to the fixed liabilities, the long-term money. (These terms are explained in Figure 7.1.)

Fig. 7.1 Guide to ten key financial terms

Return
Net profit (usually before tax and sometimes before interest charges where levied by a parent company on a subsidiary)

Capital employed
Fixed assets plus working capital

Fixed assets
Money tied up in land, buildings, plant and machinery

Current assets
Money tied up in stock, work in progress, debtors, cash, etc.

Current liabilities
Money owed in the short term, e.g. creditors, overdraft, tax, dividends

Working capital
Current assets minus current liabilities

Fixed liabilities
The long-term money in the company, i.e. shareholder's equity, long-term loans, retained profits

Margin
Sales revenue minus cost of goods sold

Balance sheet
The overall statement of a company's position at one moment in time, usually at the end of the financial year, showing the sources of the money in the company (fixed liabilities + current liabilities) and how it is deployed (fixed assets + current assets)

Profit and loss account
A statement showing the results of a company's trading in the period, indicating revenue, expenditure and thus profit

---

149

This primary ratio of R/CE is a function of two secondary ratios, return (R) on sales (S) multiplied by turnover of the capital employed, the number of times the capital employed is utilized in generating sales revenue. Thus the basic profit mechanism of the company can be represented:

$$\frac{R}{CE} = \frac{R}{S} \times \frac{S}{CE}$$

This equation, in turn, depends upon other ratios. A change in return on sales must be due to a movement in one or any combination of the following four factors: sales volume; price; cost; product mix.

For example, a potentially dangerous future position can easily be masked if figures such as sales volume and revenue are viewed in isolation. If volume increases have been achieved by price-cutting or revenue expanded by selling more of the low-margin products, then ratios analysis will help identify the concomitant risk to profitability.

A change in capital turnover will be caused by either a rise or fall in the utilization of fixed assets and/or working capital. Furthermore, for example, if the turnover of working capital has altered then it must be as a result of relative change in the relationships of current assets and/or current liabilities to sales. Analysis of capital utilization in this way can help reveal that the apparently successful sales campaign has created such a build-up in debtors that profitability has suffered.

By this process of reasoning a ratio hierarchy can be developed down to departmental detail which will analyse total company operations. Figure 7.2 shows a typical ratio chart.

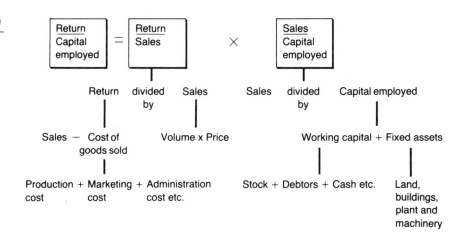

Fig. 7.2 A typical ratio chart

Identifying the profit input of marketing

A ratio tree covers total company operations and can be used to identify marketing's contribution to profit-making. Most sales and marketing will recognize their responsibilities in the R/S portion of the equation; this is a natural development from the sales-oriented approach. In this half of the hierarchy, the ratios can be employed very effectively to analyse the reasons for performance change. It is usually illuminating to identify the relative importance of volume, price, cost and mix changes, particularly in those companies which seem to believe that the solution to every profitability problem is to increase volume.

Some problems are inherent here. For example it is surprising how few sales managers clearly recognise their inputs into the S/CE part of the mechanism.

As Figure 7.2 shows, two of the major components of working capital are stocks and debtors. Although the sales manager may not directly control credit granting, debt collection and stock availability, indubitably his policies must have an impact on them and thence on the profitability of the company. Interestingly there is a paradox here. If the sales manager wishes to increase his sales volume, two of the tactics he might well use are immediate ex-stock delivery and generous credit terms. Whilst such inducements will almost certainly increase sales and probably the R/S half of the equation, they could have a disastrous effect on the sales/capital employed area, leading ultimately to lower profitability in terms of the ratio R/CE.

This quick analysis of the marketing input to the profit mechanism immediately shows up areas of responsibility that need to be defined:

151

- Who should set stock levels?
- Who should control credit when it is used as a promotional tool?
- Is the product mix sufficiently specified and controlled?

It should be possible in every company to identify which managers are to be responsible for which ratios. That alone is a major step forward in planning and controlling the business, if only because it highlights the interfunctional conflicts that must be resolved. For example, if the production manager is wholly responsible for finished stock levels he will tend to keep them low to save cost. The sales manager given that authority may well decide to increase both the range and the depth of the stocks in order to capitalize on every sales opportunity. Usually some compromise must be reached in the light of the impact on the overall profitability.

The people element

All the above has been concerned with the numbers. Make no mistake the numbers are important. In commercial firms, profit is the driving force; it not only pays the salaries and wages, it provides a return for the shareholders and the wherewithal (which may, of course, be augmented by borrowing) to finance future growth through investment. But business, and therefore marketing, is about people. Take the people out of any business and you are left with very little; certainly with very little that is going to do anything of its own volition.

Two areas of people are worth a word. First, those who are in marketing. The range is considerable, from the salesman calling on a customer on the other side of the world, to a computer expert designing marketing control systems and an adman 'dreaming up' the next creative idea that will make future advertising work effectively. All need their own talents and skills, though all must share a common customer orientation.

152

What about the marketing director? And director is right because marketing is, or should be, a top management function. Who is likely to do this job, and what kind of person is likely to do it best?

The 'classic' marketing person has probably come up the organisational ladder through one principal tactical task area – research, product development, pricing, distribution or the communication areas: public relations, advertising and/or promotion, or selling. They must know something of them all, the priorities vary but some are universal. Surely all marketing people need to be persuasive communicators, most will have some direct customer contact. And, while it is perhaps impossible for them to be able to do everything, they must be expert in key areas. They must be a good manager. Usually numbers of people are involved in the marketing process, and they must be found, developed and a plan and organisation worked out for them. They must be controlled, motivated; and all this and more takes up just as much time, and demands just as much skill, as that required of any manager leading a group of people and responsible for achieving results *through* them.

But marketing also needs direction. Whoever wears 'the marketing hat' has to be able to see the broad view, the long term. They must be a strategist not only with vision but able to put together all the elements necessary to implement a marketing plan which sets out *how* to achieve chosen objectives; and do so in a way that recognises other functions within the company and works constructively with them.

What else? There is a need for numeracy, decision making, and various interactive skills – negotiation, presentational ability, and communications in every sense is vital. (Many of these may only reach the appropriate standard through training – marketing people are not born able to do this range of things, though they may well have inherent creativity.) They must work systematically, spotting opportunities, collecting and analysing information, and taking and seeing through action that will achieve their aims, yet balance all this with the other intentions of the organisation and others in it. It is no easy task; and in a company of any size several – often many – people are involved; it is a team effort and the net result must creatively seek success in the market place and do so on a continuous basis.

153

None of this can happen in isolation. Not even a marketing person is an island and throughout this text it has been the intention to show how marketing interacts with other elements of the company. Some it leads, some it is supported by – all are needed. Marketing must recognise this, it has a responsibility to inform others of these links because if they work well they make it more likely that the company will thrive and meet its objectives in the market place. There is a strong case for saying that every organisation will do better if it has a marketing culture; this is a theme that is picked up in the Afterword as it provides an appropriate point on which to end this review.

IMPLICATIONS AROUND THE COMPANY (7)

Information and control

There is an old saying that information is power. Certainly in the marketing area good information, up-to-date information is invaluable to the decision making and the successful implementation of action that follows.

Without suggesting that every non-marketing person in the business appoints themselves a part time researcher to the detriment of their own job, it is worth noting that a company cannot have too many eyes and ears. Some companies use staff as a regular part of their market research. In others suggestion schemes produce informal ideas from throughout the organisation, some in the marketing area. Still others see internal groups, those on the production line perhaps, as sources of recruitment to the marketing side – as salesmen, say.

Companies can usually ask:

154

- What staff think of products, product charges, advertising and other promotional activity

- What staff think (and see) of competitive activity

- What experience staff have as customers (some will buy their own product) or as customers buying a competitor's product

Another major change in recent years has been company Annual Reports. Originally aimed at shareholders, or, more likely shareholders' accountants, they now are used specifically to inform and motivate staff. As such, drab layout and content has been replaced by something designed to be read by many levels of staff. More companies have profit sharing or share option schemes, and any success in these areas springs, in part at least, from the company's marketing success or failure.

Good communications breed co-operation, and in turn more effective or more productive activity. Take note of what is offered, in newsletters, on noticeboards, in company magazines, through the company's visible promotional activity. If you understand more of what is going on, you are more likely to be able to contribute constructively to it. And, if information is sparse – ask; better communications must be prompted by something or someone; why not you?

As a brief example, the sales manager of a publishing company, who I met on a course, complained of the information provided by the editorial side of the company about forthcoming new titles. It was from this he had to brief the sales team, and the content and format were, as he put it: 'all wrong'. Although the editor concerned was more senior and had been in the company a long time, prompted to ask them (or rather to produce an example of what would be more useful, as a guideline) he was surprised to find ready acceptance of the new suggested format. 'Why ever didn't you mention this before?' said the editor.

Such a reaction is not guaranteed, however you might be surprised how often changes can be made, if only after some debate or consultation (or argument!). One thing is certain, if nothing is said, things will remain as they are, and opportunities for improvement will be lost.

Summary

155

Remember the four questions posed in Chapter 2 in discussing planning:

- Where are we now?
- Where do we want to go?
- How will we get there?
- How will we know when we get there?

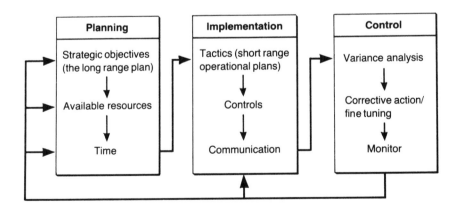

Fig. 7.3 Implementing and controlling the marketing plan

Simply, control answers the final question, and not only answers it but allows opportunity for fine-tuning of performance, a hand on the tiller to adjust course when things are not going exactly to plan and, just as important, the possibility to take advantage of changes which present, sometimes unexpected, opportunities. Thus, with this in mind, we see how important co-ordination is to the marketing process. The progression from planning to implementation to control in a continuing cycle (illustrated in Figure 7.3) is as important overall as any of the individual elements; together they make the process work. With all of this, good factual information is the basis of the best decisions, and any source of good information is to be welcomed.

IMPLICATIONS: Review and Action	
Your Job	Related Areas
POINTS TO REVIEW	POINTS TO REVIEW
POINTS TO ACTION	POINTS TO ACTION

157

Afterword

■

So, there you are, you should now (assuming you have reached this point by reading through from the beginning!) have a better understanding of the world of marketing, in concept and in its activities. We began with the 'three p's': product, price and presentation and added what is sometimes referred to as the 'fourth p': place, in the chapter on distribution.

Perhaps, we can end on the 'five c's'.

The first 'c' of marketing is **customer**. The whole of every aspect of marketing, the concept, the planning through to all the research, communications, and the application of every technique must focus on the customer. The customer is King, as the saying has it: he is ultimately also the piper that calls the tune.

The second is **continuous.** Marketing is not an option, a bolt-on activity, or for moments when 'time allows'; it must be present all the time as the company goes about its business. Indeed, without marketing there is a good chance it will *not* go about its business, at least not for long.

Next, **co-ordinated**; unless the many and various techniques of marketing are made to act together their effectiveness will be diluted. The different factors, sales and advertising to pick two obvious ones, are not alternatives; it is likely that both are necessary. When, how, and how much they interrelate and overlap is down to the skill of those involved. Often this on-going need for co-ordination is made more difficult by the number of people involved, usually spread across many departments and, sometimes, spread geographically – at its broadest across the world. Marketing is, in the true sense, a management function.

The fourth is **creativity**. Above all marketing must differentiate, and, in what seem to be ever more competitive times, this is a challenging task. It is this combination of competitiveness and creativity which makes marketing so dynamic. It is not an exact science, and many of the variables are external. One never knows, for instance, what a competitor will do next. So, however the necessary creativity shows itself, through product innovation, clever (or more important, persuasive and memorable) advertising, or special attention to some aspect of service; it must always be there bringing something new to bear to combat unpredictable competitive pressures.

And, last, and of special relevance to this book on marketing, **culture.** Marketing is, above all, dependent on people. Not only the people in marketing, the researchers, the marketing and brand managers, sales managers and account executives, but the many others throughout any organisation who are, in fact, involved in some way with the process. Some are involved in an obvious way like those in customer care; anyone who handles a customer enquiry (or complaint), provides information, technical support or after-sales service contributes. Others, as we have seen, are a little more removed, but can still contribute. What is more, senior management in any organisation should not only recognise this, but work to ensure everyone contributes knowingly and positively, better still, that as they do so they understand why and get satisfaction from the contribution they are able to make.

The starting point of all this is understanding of the company and its customers in a marketing context – and how it affects each individual. If this book helps with that process of understanding, then it will have made a practical contribution; because ultimately a marketing orientated culture can help generate success and produce the profits which pay everyone's salary – and which can only ever come from the market outside the organisation.

Note

Reading this book may have prompted you to think about how your job links with the marketing area and process. It may even have given you reason to believe that you can do more to assist the marketing activity. This may be in terms of an immediate idea. If so, make a note, tell someone or, if appropriate, start an on-going dialogue – communications can be given a boost from either end.

Alternatively you may be in a position from which a systematic review of the linkage could produce more than an isolated idea. In this case, the Appendix which follows – and which is largely in checklist form – may be a stimulus to that kind of review, whether this is something you do, or something you do with others from your own side of the business, or from marketing; or both. The questions posed are not intended to be comprehensive, but they will give a reminder of key areas and a flavour of the depth and range of issues involved.

161

Appendix
Making marketing work

■

Earlier in the text marketing was referred to as as much art as science. This is certainly true. While elements of marketing are quantitative, and there is a need to operate on the basis of solid data where possible, there is also a creative area involved. Some of that is in the obvious areas of, say, advertising where a clever and original campaign can make all the difference. But it is also inherent to the overall approach; in other words the process of managing marketing needs to be itself creative.

This appendix examines briefly some of the factors that con-tribute to this.

In recent years there has been some examination, indeed some research, of just what it is that distinguishes the more successful companies from their less successful rivals. A number of books have been published and two are worth a mention here.

The first is *In Search of Excellence* (Peters and Waterman – Harper & Row). This isolated eight factors the authors regarded as key:

– a bias for action: this simply means being action orientated. This can be easier said than done in some organisations, and the moral is that the organisation structure and the hierarchy must allow the right people to get together, not simply to plan but to prompt action as and when necessary. This is vital in marketing where the market favours those who are quick on their feet.

– closeness to customers: this should go without saying, but some companies do operate either with inadequate research or with an introspective approach that ignores the detail of customer view; nowhere is this more important perhaps than in customer service.

– **autonomy and entrepreneurship:** innovation is necessary in many aspects of marketing activity, certainly in the development of new products and services (or their rejuvenation) and organisation must allow, indeed encourage, this process.

– **hands-on value driven:** in other words management – senior management – must be involved throughout and understand and propagate the beliefs on which the operation is based; mission statements must be operational documents.

– **stick to the knitting:** this phrase refers to concentration on the key issues, pursuing the line in what we know best; many companies flounder because they dissipate effort and end up doing nothing really well because they are trying to progress too many strategies at once.

– **simple form, lean staff:** simplicity seems to work best, simple rather than complex line structures, flatter organisations with few levels of staff and, above all, clarity of who does what and how everything works together – without any attendant and unnecessary bureaucracy.

– **loose tight properties:** management control must be absolute on those matters that are key to business success; certain information in any business must be known promptly, accurately and clearly if decision making can follow on an informed basis.

– **productivity through people:** people do business not organisations, so those that respect the individual, develop and utilise their full potential, do better.

Despite the American phrases, the sentiments expressed above make good sense. All relate directly or indirectly to the way an organisation relates to its markets and thus affect particularly the marketing side of activities. A British book along similar lines, *The Winning Streak* (Goldsmith & Clutterbuck) highlighted a not dissimilar list: **leadership, autonomy, control, involvement, market orientation, zero-basing** (defining similar areas to stick to the knitting), **integrity.**

All reinforce the view, certainly inherent in what has been

written in this book, that successful marketing does not just happen; it needs working at, it needs time, attention and creativity.

So finally here we will end on a check list note, because ultimately what makes marketing succeed is attention to detail, constant review and finetuning of action – against a background of the factors mentioned above and elsewhere – systematically reviewing all the key areas of marketing and the things that affect it to ensure that it is not only set up in a way that will make success more likely, but stays organised for maximum effectiveness. The questions that follow therefore are what the marketing side of your organisation should be investigating; they may also provide a way of doublechecking what you can contribute to the process.

Logically we start by looking externally:

165

ENVIRONMENTAL FACTORS

Economic/political
– what is affecting our market and customers?

– what is affecting our costs?

– what are the implications for our pricing policy?

– are changes necessary to corporate policy?

Environmental
A more recent and increasingly important area:
– are there dangers to image?

– are there opportunities arising from prevailing thinking?

Social/legislative
– is legislation affecting promotion, price, product or any other area of marketing activity?

– are changes going to affect our staff or customers?

Technology
– how will the various technological changes inherent in the modern world affect products, customers and how we operate?

The net result of all these questions is to ascertain whether the company's philosophy, culture, planning and organisation is appropriate to the situation in which it must work now and is likely to have to work in future.

MARKET FACTORS
– are customer needs changing?

– is the market changing in nature?

– is the customer group aimed at changing in structure or location?

– is the demographic basis of the market changing?

DISTRIBUTIVE FACTORS
– are ways of accessing the market changing?

– are there changes in the area of physical distribution?

– are the channels and intermediaries through whom business is done changing in nature or requirements?

COMPETITORS
– is enough known about direct competitors?

– what about indirect competition?

– are new competitive pressures on the horizon?

MARKETING ACTIVITY
This is not, as we have seen, static. It needs constant review and change. So questions must be asked of current practice on a continuous basis in the following areas:

Customer attitudes
– are potential customers well identified?

– are their needs understood?

– how well do current offerings satisfy those needs?

– what image do they have of the company?

– what view do they take of competitors?

Corporate intention

– is the relationship between marketing and required profit clear?

– is financial performance measured against competitors?

– is management able to monitor financial performance in a way that monitors progress and enables both corrective action to be taken and opportunities grasped?

Product/service

– is the status of the product reviewed regularly?

– is its position in its life-cycle understood?

– is product range satisfactory in extent?

– is a product development system in place?

Price

– is price market related?

– is pricing policy reviewed regularly?

– is pricing structure (terms, discounts etc) right?

167

Distribution

– does current policy give the access required?

– are outlets managed, dealt with and motivated effectively?

– is physical distribution method cost effective?

– is distribution regarded as a variable just like other marketing variables?

Next, the various promotional techniques must be constantly monitored to ascertain how they are performing.

Public relations

– who should be communicated with?

– what do they know of the company already?

– what image should be presented?

– what feedback is regularly obtained?

Advertising

– who should be communicated with?

– are messages appropriate and persuasive?

– is what is done objective orientated rather than fashion?

Sales promotion
– is it clear at which points of the marketing process sales promotion is appropriate?

– is what is done organised towards specific goals?

– is promotion organised as an integral part of the mix?

Selling
– is the detail of the sales job well defined?

– are all methods of personal contact being used cost-effectively (eg teleselling)?

– is the sales resource well trained and managed?

– is the sales team appropriately deployed?

The mix
– are all aspects of the promotional and sales mix integrated?

– is sufficient time and effort being put into planning and organising all of this compared with implementing activity?

CORPORATE MATTERS
Everything in marketing works better if it takes place against a background in which the company overall is clear in its intentions:

– is it clearly defined what business it is in?

– are profit goals spelt out in terms that relate to the various levels and divisions of the organisation?

– is there a plan, which sets out objectives and specifies the implications in terms of specific, timed action plans for all those involved?

In addition, there are three further areas of review that are corporate in scope and which need clarity and regular review:

Marketing planning
– is there a plan?

– is there a satisfactory system for producing and updating the plan?

– are the right people involved in the process?

– does any necessary documentation assist rather than restrict the thinking involved?

– is the whole process constructive and does it prompt creativity?

– is the plan communicated, indeed does it stimulate constructive communication around the organisation?

– is the plan regularly evaluated against subsequent events?

– does it link to individual action and assessment?

– does it work as a true operating document (rather than gathering dust on the shelf)?

Marketing organisation

– is everyone involved in marketing organised so as to maximise effectiveness?

– does the organisational structure ensure the action that is required happens promptly and constructively?

– are individual jobs well defined and responsibilities understood?

169

– is everything in marketing based on sound experience and training?

– are the supporting systems arranged to help the activity or does administration apply an unintentional brake on what is being done?

– is information necessary for marketing available, up to date and appropriately and promptly circulated?

– are communications around the firm as they should be, both within any marketing department and more widely around the company so that *everyone* involved in whatever way understands how they assist the marketing activity and results?

– is motivation an asset to marketing initiative (or a drain)?

Marketing control

– is what constitutes success well defined?

– are measurement devices in place?

– are all cause-effect factors understood and monitored?

– are management information and management information systems sufficiently market based?

– is there a focus on key results areas?

Overall marketing is a senior management responsibility. Whoever runs the marketing side of corporate activity needs experience, needs to take a strategic view (where are we going?), while being a good tactician (how do we get there?). It demands a scientific approach, one that starts by identifying opportunities, collects and analyses data, formulates solutions, tests, implements and does so ever watchful for changes in market conditions. It is not easy. It is one of the most challenging roles in many organisations.

It must involve good management, creatively applied and has as much of the art about it as science. And it must do so creatively if it is to continue to attract consumer attention amongst no doubt strident and creative competitors. In one sense you might think that everything that could reasonably be done has been done, however marketing people seem to continue to find ways to ring the changes. In advertising for instance, consider how dated the advertising of a few years ago looks; yet at the time it was considered right up to date. The same is true of other methodology, who would have imagined before it occurred that coal or potatoes would be sold in petrol filling stations, or that advertisements on the television would use stories running like serials – or that people would follow them so avidly! But it is ultimately easy to measure. Marketing must at the end of the day deliver profit.* Profit can only be generated outside the organisation, it is that that pays the wages and salaries, that enables the company to develop and grow.

There are no magic formulae, no panaceas. Marketing is judged by achievement rather than activity. For example, an advertisement may win awards, but sell little. A plan may look good on

---

*This is not, in fact, strictly true, at least in an exclusive sense. Some organisations are non-profit making (intentionally that is), but still regard themselves as being marketing orientated and using marketing techniques. This would apply to a charity for example; here the end result is not profit but a surplus that can go towards whatever cause the charity promotes. This kind of process is referred to as social marketing. In addition certain marketing techniques are used in other fields, the advertising that accompanies an election for instance – though whether you feel this has anything to do with consumer need is a moot point!

paper, but achieve few of its objectives. So marketing must work continuously and use all the resources at its disposal to increase the chances of success in markets where customers are increasingly fickle and change is the order of the day. Ultimately, however, it is the people in any organisation are one of its most important resources, and from a marketing perspective this includes people in many parts of the company, at many levels and in many functions. Many people can play their part in helping make marketing work. The checklist above, or other similar thinking you may be able to bring to bear, may prompt ideas that can make a difference in your organisation.

If so, perhaps you can play an increased part in ensuring marketing success; as was said earlier, marketing is neither easy nor certain – nor should it be proud; from wherever help is available it should be used. What matters is that the totality of ideas works and produces the results looked for in the market place not where those ideas come from.

171

Postscript

(because, though marketing is a serious business,
it should also be fun.)

∎

If a man goes to a party and says to a woman that she needs a man and should come home with him; that's marketing. If he stands on a chair and declares to the assembled company his expertise and availability in matters of love; that is advertising. If he tells the woman he is the world's greatest lover and that she should come home with him at once; that's selling. And if she comes to him and says she hears he is the world's greatest lover will he please come home with her; that's public relations. And a good trick for those who can do it.

Patrick Forsyth, *Everything you need to know about Marketing* (Kogan Page).

Index

■